The SUN
Still RISES

Advance Praise for *The Sun Still Rises*

"What a gem of a book. I read it in one sitting and will be sending copies to women I love. And the reason is that Nora Tubbs Tisdale is exactly the person I want to be our prayer partner and travel companion through the middle seasons: wise, tender, compassionate, and filled with joy."

> —ANNA CARTER FLORENCE, Peter Marshall Professor of Preaching, Columbia Theological Seminary, and author of *Preaching as Testimony*

"In *The Sun Still Rises*, Nora Tisdale has written a true accounting of a genuine faith as it is lived out in daily life. She knows that we can't avoid the hard and messy, but she shows us how to reflect on them. Smart, searching, and deeply real, Nora Tisdale is the perfect guide to help us find meaning in our often-scattered, confusing lives."

> —NORA GALLAGHER, best-selling author of four memoirs, including *Moonlight Sonata at the Mayo Clinic*, and a novel, *Changing Light*

"As a pastor who often finds herself running from task to event to meeting, etc., I found that Nora's book provided me a sacred pause. I noticed that each time I finished reading a meditation, I would be breathing more deeply. Nora might have written this book as her own expression of the Jubilee Year, but by doing so, she shares moments of Jubilee with us all. And I, a middle-aged pastor myself, am deeply grateful for it!"

> —SHANNON J. KERSHNER, pastor, Fourth Presbyterian Church, Chicago

"I know Nora Tubbs Tisdale as preacher, professor, author, and colleague in the world of practical theology. Her particular voice has mentored my preaching and pastoral care. In this collection of meditations, Nora is a wise guide, a coach, a lyrical and insightful observer of her life, of the passage of time and the coming of age. Reading her wonderful prose, we must look anew at our own journeys and the wisdom that comes at every turn. This is a beautiful, moving book, one to pick up again and again. Brava, Nora!"

—JACQUI LEWIS, Senior Minister, Middle Collegiate Church, Manhattan, and author of *The Power of Stories: A Guide for Leading Multi-Racial, Multi-Cultural Congregations*, and the children's book, *You Are So Wonderful!*

"Written by a master teacher and preacher who has been tutored in the classroom of the Spirit, Nora Tubbs Tisdale offers every reader the gift of encountering God through these meditations. From the joy of Jubilee to the pain of cancer and facing one's mortality, Tisdale tells the truth about God and life. It is raw, real, righteous, and resurrecting. Faith is the thread that holds these literary pearls together. Whoever reads this book will walk away from these pages in hope knowing that 'the sun still rises.'"

—LUKE POWERY, Dean of Duke Chapel, Associate Professor of Homiletics at Duke University, and author of *Dem Dry Bones: Preaching, Death, and Hope*

"We all yearn for and search for spiritual treasures to help us along the way. *The Sun Still Rises* is one of those spiritual treasures that sustains and encourages us on the journey."

—EMILIE M. TOWNES, Dean and the E. Rhodes and Leona B. Carpenter Professor of Womanist Ethics and Society, Vanderbilt Divinity School, and author of *Womanist Ethics and the Cultural Production of Evil* and *In a Blaze of Glory: Womanist Spirituality as Social Witness*

LEONORA TUBBS TISDALE

The SUN
Still RISES

Meditations on
Faith at Midlife

WJK WESTMINSTER
JOHN KNOX PRESS
LOUISVILLE · KENTUCKY

First edition
Published by Westminster John Knox Press
Louisville, Kentucky

17 18 19 20 21 22 23 24 25 26 — 10 9 8 7 6 5 4 3 2 1

Book design by Drew Stevens
Cover design by Allison Taylor

Library of Congress Cataloging-in-Publication Data

Names: Tisdale, Leonora Tubbs, author.
Title: The sun still rises : meditations on faith at midlife / Leonora Tubbs Tisdale.
Description: Louisville, KY : Westminster John Knox Press, 2017.
Identifiers: LCCN 2016041538 (print) I LCCN 2016048631 (ebook) I ISBN 9780664262600 (pbk. : alk. paper) I ISBN 9781611647969 (ebk.)
Subjects: LCSH: Middle-aged persons — Religious life — Meditations. I Christianity — Meditations.
Classification: LCC BV4579.5 .T57 2017 (print) I LCC BV4579.5 (ebook) I DDC 242/.64 — dc23
LC record available at https://lccn.loc.gov/2016041538

Most Westminster John Knox Press books are available at special quantity discounts when purchased in bulk by corporations, organizations, and special-interest groups. For more information, please e-mail SpecialSales@wjkbooks.com.

For my wonderful company of women friends

who grace my life at every stage

with wisdom, kindness, encouragement, and good humor.

How blessed I am to have you in my life!

CONTENTS

Disciplines and Gifts of the Spirit

The Gift of Friendship and Family

FOREWORD

"I think midlife is when the universe gently places her hands upon your shoulders, pulls you close, and whispers in your ear: I'm not screwing around. It's time. Courage and daring are coursing through you. You were made to live and love with your whole heart."
— *Brené Brown*

Nobody knows for sure who said it first, but it's been repeated many times since: youth is wasted on the young. At first it sounds like a bitterly tinged, nursing-home conversation starter, but perhaps there's some truth there. Life is a great teacher. Sometimes only reflection and experience allow us to see the depth and power and treasure of the gift of life. And when we begin to recognize the new vantage point from which we see the world, the lens of time and experience prioritizes what we know to be true and important, and we know — it's time.

In these beautiful reflections from the perspective of midlife, a seasoned pastor's voice reminds us that integrating body and soul, savoring the gifts of life, and asking what mark we are making on this world become our principle work at this point along the journey. Midlife is when we begin living more fully and intentionally into who we are and who we hope to become with the gifts of the past informing the next season of life.

Beginning with jubilee—the exercise of resting from frantic achievement and reflecting on the life around and within us—some consistent themes for reflection begin to emerge. By skillfully parsing these threads that weave their way through the years over and over again, we're invited to consider them again: hope, unexpected grace, beauty, questions, and love.

You'll soon realize that the devotional reflections collected here do not limit themselves to a cursory glance at common themes of human life. They go deeper, into the harder and more painful experiences that we collect as life unfolds. Living with a deadly disease—cancer—through the eyes of the author recalls that midlife invites us to savor the gifts of living we may not have appreciated before. Nora Tisdale's frank and honest reflections on recognizing the brevity of life, in realities too close to ignore, helped me to realize that one of the precious gifts of midlife is the practice of savoring all that has been and all that is, life in its sweetest and most immediate expressions.

Considering the precious and bittersweet gift of family as it shifts and changes at this point in life was another invitation I couldn't ignore. What is the soul work I undertake as I learn to say good-bye forever to dear ones who pass on, and say good-bye just a little bit to children who grow up and into their own lives?

Halfway through the adventure of human life, there's no denying that life is charted in the landscape of gray and shadow questions, so much more frequently than in black-and-white assurances. These reflections claim those shadows as beautiful perspective in a life well-lived and invite me to ask again: What do I hold most dear and claim most ardently as truth?

Welcome to a companion who walks along the journey, naming the pain and breathtaking beauty of midlife. Through her words you will claim the gift of your own life and celebrate the courage it takes to live and love with your whole heart. It's time.

Amy Butler
Senior Minister
The Riverside Church
New York

ACKNOWLEDGMENTS

The person who first taught me to love devotional literature is my mom, Leonora "Lee" Cousar Tubbs. From the
earliest days of my childhood to the present day, my mom
has arisen earlier than the rest of our family to pray for
us. With her coffee cup, Bible, and prayer journal close at
hand, Mom enters into a time of deep meditation, reflection, and prayer each and every day. Through the years
she has also engaged many different devotional books, or
books that lend themselves to devotional reading. Mom,
a serious lay biblical scholar (her shelves at the retirement home where she now resides are lined with the latest
up-to-date commentaries), does not like pabulum for her
early morning reading. She gravitates toward books with
theological depth and spiritual substance. She would be
the first to attest that her morning time with God has been
transformative for her. And each of us, her four children,
can attest as well to the incredible difference her prayers
have made in our lives.

In my middle adulthood, I have joined Mom (now
eighty-eight) as an early morning pray-er. She and I use
the same prayer journal these days to record our thanksgivings and our intercessions. She and I trade ideas for
good devotional reading. And she and I are both fans of

the poems of my former Yale colleague, Thomas Troeger, whose deeply insightful and faithful poetry Mom refers to as her "devotional dessert." She is my first inspiration for this book, and I am more grateful to her than I can say for a lifetime of prayers, faithful witness, and shared wisdom.

The second inspiration for this book is my beloved spouse, Alfred. He is decidedly *not* a morning person, but he has been my encourager, soul mate, and best friend for the past forty-three years. He too is a person of prayer and of deep spirituality. And he was the person who, when I decided to leave a safe and secure job and leap into the unknown of Jubilee time over fifteen years ago, blessed, encouraged, and supported me every step of the way. He is the partner who continues to make my journey with God joyful—even on the most challenging days.

Third, I want to thank some colleagues who have been significant encouragers along the way. Tom Troeger, my colleague in teaching preaching at Yale Divinity School for nine years before his retirement in 2015, read an early draft of this work, saw its potential, and spurred me on with his enthusiasm at times when I doubted myself. He is one of the most creative and imaginative preachers, teachers, poets, and hymn writers I know, and also one of the kindest human beings. My dear friend and colleague Jan Holton has also been a great support. When I doubted whether people even read devotional literature anymore, it was the image of Jan reading devotions to her mother (now deceased) over the phone each evening that renewed my purpose and commitment in writing. The author Nora Gallagher, who is a member of our divinity school's advisory council and a new friend to me, also offered me encouragement, wise counsel, and savvy insight at a juncture when I needed it most. Thank you, Nora! I could not have had a better or more trusted editor than David Maxwell at Westminster John Knox Press. He not only believed in this book from his first reading of it but also offered much-needed counsel along the way about its content, organizational structure, title, and other matters (including what to leave on the cutting room floor!) — such counsel always offered with a large dose of generous kindness. I am also grateful to Yale Divinity School and to its dean, Gregory Sterling, for the sabbatical that allowed me the time I needed to pull this book together.

Finally, a word of gratitude to the women who would not let the dream of this book die: Mary (aka "Trauma") Eaddy Petrakis, Helen Keller, Jacquelyn Deberry O'Dell, Margaret McEver Cobb, and Nadia Rasheed Black. We are quite a sextet: half of us Democrats, half of us Republicans; serving in a diversity of vocations; all people of faith, who, despite our differences, have hung together and supported one another for the past forty-seven years — ever since we bonded during our first year in college. For a number of years now these women have asked me at our annual gatherings: "Where is that devotional book you promised to write?" Well, dear friends, here it is. And it is to you, along with a company of other equally wonderful and much-beloved women friends, that I have dedicated this book. How blessed I have been to have you all in my life, at midlife and at all the other ages and stages as well.

INTRODUCTION

Tucked away in the biblical book of Leviticus (probably one of the least read books in the Bible!) are instructions to the Israelites to observe a Year of Jubilee every fiftieth year.* The entire year was intended to be Sabbath time during which the Israelites were to let the land lie fallow, to let their indentured slaves go free, to return land to its rightful owners, and to forgive all debts.

Imagine! An entire year devoted to release, renewal, replenishment, and liberation. It was such a radical idea that biblical scholars debate how regularly the Israelites actually practiced it. Yet at its heart we glimpse the wisdom of a God who knows that there are times in life when we mortals need such extended seasons of Sabbath and release—for both our own flourishing and the flourishing of God's entire creation.

While I know that the original Jubilee Year was intended to be observed by an entire community, it began occurring to me at midlife that what I individually craved

---

*See Leviticus 25:8–55. Since the instructions for the Jubilee Year are that it is to be observed every 7 × 7 years, it is uncertain whether the year was actually meant to be observed in the forty-ninth or fiftieth year. For the sake of this book's focus on midlife challenges, I have chosen to go with the fiftieth-year hypothesis.

more than anything else was some Jubilee time for myself. By that point in life I had been working for a number of years in a job that had worn me out, worn me down, and robbed me of the joy of my vocation. Spiritually speaking, I often found myself clinging to the promise of the psalmist: "The LORD . . . shall preserve thy soul" (Ps. 121:7 KJV). I was seriously in need of soul preservation.

On the home front, I was doing what many women of my age and stage find themselves doing at midlife: juggling the many demands of parenting, pursuing a career, and keeping a household running—and often feeling that I was failing miserably at one or more of those tasks. Since I had been engaged in that juggling act for almost twenty years at that point, I was also tired. Very tired.

And so, at age fifty I took a leap in faith, resigned my tenured faculty job at a Protestant seminary, and embarked on my own Year of Jubilee.

This was definitely a risky venture, since at the time my pastor husband and I had one child in college and another on the way to college. Financially, my job resignation put a serious strain on our family. Vocationally, I wondered if anyone would ever hire me again after this precipitous move. And as a parent, I worried about what my decision would mean for my children's educational future.

But I was also privileged in ways that many, many other folk are not—especially given that I had a working spouse who could keep bread on our table and a roof over our heads and who supported me in this decision each step of the way.

While my own Jubilee time turned out to be over a year in length, I am well aware that few people can afford to take an entire year off work. Nor do we all need to do so.

But I am convinced of two things. The first is that we all need some "Jubilee" time for renewal and reflection in our lives—whether we grab it early in the morning before our household awakes, in the car on our way to work, through occasional day-long retreats, or through more radical measures. Claiming Sabbath time in our lives is often not as much about gaining more time as it is about prioritizing the time we have. So I hope you will view this book as an invitation to reflect creatively on how you might incorporate such Jubilee time in the rhythms of your own life, whatever they may be.

The second conviction I have is that midlife is an especially fertile season for getting off life's treadmill and taking stock, to make sure the direction in which we are heading is the one in which we want to keep going. For many people at midlife, the pace of life is so frenetic and full that we have almost no time to "let the land lie fallow." But it is especially at that juncture at life that we need to ask some hard questions of God and of ourselves:

— Am I on a vocational path that gives me deep meaning and joy, and if not, what other paths might I pursue?
— What are those things that feed my soul and spirit — rather than depleting them — and how might I expose myself to more of them?
— What are the debts I need to forgive, and how might I begin and continue the hard work of forgiveness?
— How can the losses I am confronted with at this stage in life — whether they be death, the ending of a relationship, job loss, or an empty nest — open me to the new possibilities that God might have in store for my life?

My own Jubilee Year involved a lot of early-morning prayer and sun-porch sitting. (We had a sunporch in our home at that time, which became my personal sanctuary.) I knew that prayer was going to be critical to my healing and renewal, so I embraced it for as long as I desired each day. I also limited my reading to books that fed my soul and spirit. Consequently, I read a lot of poetry, a number of volumes on feminist spirituality (including Sister Joan Chittister's entire corpus), and books that nurtured creative aspects of my being (especially books on creative writing). In addition I took on only those tasks that I truly wanted to take on: no "oughts" or "shoulds" allowed. Among the new activities I embraced were forming and leading a group called FRAWG—the Feminist Reading and Worship Group—at my local church (with an acronym like FRAWG, how could anyone accuse of us being "angry feminists"?) and volunteering at a mission and outreach center of our church where mothers who had been referred by social service organizations came to secure diapers, baby clothes, formula, and other items. Hearing the stories of these women survivors—many of them recent immigrants to the United States—was not only inspirational but also pivotal for helping me see my own very privileged life and its struggles within a larger perspective.

During the early months of my Jubilee Year, I began writing some of the meditations that eventually found their way into this book. I continued that practice off and on for the next fourteen years—writing especially during seasons when I was facing major life challenges, when I was overwhelmed by joy and gratitude, or when I simply had the time and space and inspiration to do so.

At first I wrote both as a way of expressing my newfound freedom from academia (I could write anything I wanted, and in any way that I wanted!) and as a form of self-therapy (to help me work through the deep woundedness of the previous work years and to try to make some sense of them). I also wrote as a way of sticking my feet back in the water since, along with losing the joy of teaching, I had lost the joy of my first vocational love, preaching. I found that writing these briefer reflections allowed me to do what I loved best about sermon writing: to reflect on ordinarily life in relation to what the Scriptures tell us about God and faith.

Finally, I wrote because I sensed the Holy Spirit prompting me to do so. As I would sit on that sunporch in the early mornings, praying and reading and, as I liked to put it, "wasting time with God," times would often come when I sensed the Spirit urging me to go to the computer and record the insights of the morning. The writing became a way of transitioning from my formal prayer time into the other activities of the day.

The Christian faith has been bedrock for me throughout my life, that one sure thing on which I can stake my existence and out of which I seek to interpret all that happens within it. So quite naturally, these writings are about not just my own life but how to make sense of life—with all its paradoxes and challenges—in light of that faith. The faith I speak of here is not static or simplistic or exclusivist. It is a faith open to ever-expanding understandings of God and nature and the world, and that does not always try to tie things up in neat theological packages. Faith is messy, like everyday life. And my own faith consistently looks to the biblical witness, and to the triune God revealed there, as a lens through which to make sense of life with, for, and in God.

But faith is also eternally hopeful. And my own sincere desire is that this book might help people to reflect more deeply on the messy life experiences they are going through and to find God and the hope of the gospel in the midst of them.

This book's title, *The Sun Still Rises*, reflects the nature of Christian hope. It was a mantra I first embraced during my year of battling cancer, as I would sit out on my sunporch early each morning, wrapped in a quilt, praying, and waiting for the sun to rise. No matter what life deals us, if the sun still rises anew each morning, we are given assurance that our Creator God is still in control of this world, that there is still some order and regularity to the ways of the universe, and that we can place our lives into God's safe keeping. The title also echoes resurrection themes and trust in the rising of the "Son of Righteousness," who walks with us into the long nights of life's heartbreaks and tragedies, comforting and consoling us, while also holding before us the promised dawn of a new day to come.

I am certainly not the only person who, at midlife—loosely defined as forty-five to sixty-five years old—has gone through job loss, the quest for new vocational and personal identity, or a battle with life-threatening illness. Nor am I the only person who rediscovered at midlife new delight in nature, new satisfaction in reconnecting with old friends, or new joy in growing older with my beloved spouse while embracing the marvelous new vocation of grandparenting. I am also not the only woman who has wrestled with patriarchy in the workplace, with war and its ethical challenges, with how to be a good mother to adult children, or with life during and after breast cancer.

Stages of midlife faith development are reflected here—not in the sequential way some scholars in faith development describe them—but in the messy way in which mature adults go through a series of events and life situations that can either make us stronger or wear us down—and sometimes do both simultaneously. While I'm not sure any of us ordinarily wakes up in the morning thinking, "Wow, I'm growing in faith and wisdom!" we can sometimes look back on our lives and see God's hand in the patterns of our lives and see how, slowly but surely, our mettle has been tested and our faith has been strengthened through the ups and downs we have been through with God.

This book is a hybrid: part memoir—as I chronicle fourteen years of my life (ages fifty to sixty-four) and its struggles and celebrations, and part devotional book — as I reflect on that life through the lens of faith. Each section heading in the book indicates the ages I was when I wrote the meditations included in it. Though most of these meditations begin with a story about me and one of my life experiences, I have also tried to identify through those stories the larger issues of faith and life that confront many of us at midlife and to reflect on them from the vantage point of a thoughtful faith. I have concluded most of these meditations with a suggested Scripture reading and with questions "For Further Reflection." My hope is that my reflections will spur you to embrace your own Jubilee time, asking significant questions of yourself and of God and entering into the kind of prayerful conversation with God that can lead to new insights and revelation. Space is provided if you would like to use this book as a workbook, jotting down the answers you would make to those questions as you reflect on them.

You may read the meditations in this book in any order that you choose. If you are battling illness, you might choose to start with the meditations in the section that bears that name. If you are wrestling with vocation and vocational identity, "Jubilee Time" is a good place to begin. If you are on vacation, reveling in the beauty of nature, try starting with "Nature the Nurturer."

When I started writing this book, my two children were both in college. Now they are adults with vocations of their own. When I started writing this book, I had recently resigned my job as a tenured faculty person at a Protestant seminary to embark on my "Jubilee Year." Since that time, I have served for five years on the staff of a large New York City "avenue" church, where I ran a seminary for lay people, and for ten years on the faculty of a university divinity school, where I teach preaching. There has definitely been life after my Jubilee Year and after my year with cancer (which this book also chronicles). And I have tried to live life differently and more intentionally than I did before I embarked on these life-changing experiences.

I know that not everyone has the luxury of taking a full Year of Jubilee. But I also believe there are ways to structure our everyday lives that allow us to glimpse God's will for Jubilee in their midst and to live toward it. Most of all I believe that God wants us to live these midlife years fully, freely, and joyfully—embracing all that God has in store for us, while also facing the challenges that come our way with faith and courage.

Nora Tubbs Tisdale
Pentecost 2016

JUBILEE TIME

(WRITTEN AT AGES 50–51)

THE YEAR OF MY JUBILEE

This is the year of my Jubilee—literally, figuratively, metaphorically. This, for me, is going to be a year of freedom, release, and new possibilities. The Hebrew Scriptures talk about the celebration of such a year in the life of Israel: a year celebrated every fiftieth year, when the people were told to let the land lie fallow, to forgive those who owed them debts, and to free their slaves.

Since this is my own fiftieth year, I am exactly the right age for doing what the Bible prescribes. It is the perfect year for having as a goal nothing other than to be renewed, refreshed, reinvigorated, and replenished for whatever the future holds in store. And I am making plans to celebrate it exactly in that vein.

Slowly but surely, I have been clearing the deck of my chronically overcommitted life to make space in which to read, meditate, pray, and be still enough so that I can actually listen for God's voice in the midst of the hubbub. I am letting go of the old securities—money, title, tenure—that drive me to be perpetually responsible and productive, in order to make space for a new attitude of openness, risk, and receptivity. I am also hoping to "reinvent my life" during this year, as I cut through the layers of perpetual *doing* in order to get back in touch with the ground of my *being*, and discover anew who I am, what I believe, and what I think is worthy of the remaining years of my life.

I first embraced the possibility of Jubilee last May when I decided to resign my tenured teaching chair at a well-respected theological seminary and to leap into the unknown. While the decision was made quickly, it was not made precipitously or thoughtlessly. I had pondered it for a while.

But every time I imagined myself taking the actual leap, life's realities came crashing in around me. What would happen to my family—with one child in college and another headed that way—if I gave up the steady, guaranteed income and benefits I had worked so long to acquire at just that time in life when we needed them the most? What would happen to me if I gave up the title and job that had afforded me prestige and respect in the world of theological education and traded them in for stationery with no letterhead, a résumé with no title, a personality with no position?

I had always thought that at midlife I would not go through the crises stay-at-home moms sometimes encounter when their children go away to college and they have to reinvent themselves. I thought that when that time in life came for me, I would have a solid, steady teaching vocation full of meaning and challenge and opportunity to keep me from missing my children too much, and that my husband and I would blissfully sail into our new midlife existence together without missing a beat.

But I also have to confess that when I envisioned that future, part of what made it appealing was the fact that it did have certain parameters, certain borders around it that at least defined the field on which I would be playing. To trade away my job was like trading away all the boundary lines, leaving me free to roam in a space that was too big and too terrifying and where the possibilities of being forever lost were very real. It was scary to be cut loose from those moorings that had tethered and defined me for so long and to cast my life upon God.

But that is what I decided to do that fateful spring day.

I, of course, am not the first to take such a leap in faith. The Bible is full of stories about people who did so. Abram and Sarai were called to leave their beloved homeland and travel to a land they had never before seen, a land God would show them. All they had to sustain them on their journey was a pocket full of divine promises.

Ruth chose not to go back to the safety of her family of origin after her husband died, which would have been a far more secure choice for a widow of her day, even though her mother-in-law, Naomi, urged her to do so. Instead she boldly cast her lot with her mother-in-law and her mother-in-law's God.

The children of Israel, beneficiaries of the first Jubilee Year, followed God through a wilderness sojourn that took over forty years, in order to reach their land of promised rest and freedom. For them, freedom was a quest worth risking their all.

And so, too, have countless generations of the faithful dared to give up the safe and the secure to leap into God's unknown future.

The morning after I resigned from my job, my beloved husband awoke and eyed me warily, clearly concerned that with the breaking of dawn I might have dashed my head against the hard rock of the reality of what I had done, feeling wounded by my rashness.

But my decision had not been rash. And I had not been up early nursing my wounds, bloodied by the fall. Instead I had been sitting out in the backyard in my bathrobe, watching the sunrise from my lounge chair, rubbing my bare feet in the green grass of early spring, and noticing—for the first time—the budding forsythia around me. The sun warmed my face, as I free-fell into my season of Jubilee. And I knew that whatever the future held, it was going to be good: as good as the God who gave me the courage to leap in the first place; as good as the God who waits for us all on that large, grassy, fallow field of the future.

Scripture Reading: Leviticus 25:8–12

For Further Reflection
— Has there ever been a time in your life when you have
taken a risky leap in faith with no guarantees of a safety
net beneath you? What did you learn about God and
life and faith from doing so?
— Is there a leap you should consider taking even now?
— What would it take for you to embrace your own "Jubilee" time?

REBORN TO THE ORDINARY

Yesterday afternoon, as I was running errands in my car, I tuned in to "This American Life" on my local NPR station. I love this program, not only because of the quirky way in which it excavates real life in all its earthy richness through the stories of ordinary people, but also because of the connection it affords me with my beloved daughter, Leonora. Leonora has been a fan of this program since her high school days and has long urged me to listen to it. When I turned on the radio and heard the familiar yet unusual voice of the show's host, Ira Glass, the melancholy music that is woven throughout its segments, and the announcement that this particular show was going to be centered on telling the stories of five people who thought they were going to die and how the experience changed their lives, I was hooked.

The opening story was told by a man named Kevin Kelly who used to be a reporter, traveling the world and encountering many religions as he went.* He told of the confusion that arose in his soul about his faith and how he came to a place in life where he had no idea what he should believe, or even why he should believe at all. One night, when he was in Jerusalem covering a story related to the gathering of Jews and Christians in that city to celebrate Passover and Easter, he returned to his hostel past the posted curfew hour and was locked out. He was in a strange city with literally nowhere to lay his head.

So for hours that night, he wandered the old Holy City of Jerusalem, taking respite in the only buildings still open: some churches. Finally, he found his way into the

*Kevin Kelly, "Shoulda Been Dead: Act 1. Die in Six Months," Program 50, *This American Life*, National Public Radio, first aired on January 17, 1997. I heard a rebroadcast of the program in 2002.

Church of the Holy Sepulchre, where he spent the remaining hours until dawn resting on the mound where Jesus was supposed to have been crucified. When dawn came on Easter morning, he went to the tombs area of Jerusalem, where he joined other pilgrims who were sitting in folding chairs in front of one of the empty tombs. Suddenly, he knew in the core of his being that it was true. Jesus had risen from the dead. He began asking God what he should do with his life, now that faith had been kindled within him. And the idea that came to him was that he should live as if he were going to die in six months.

Although this young man had always thought he would do something especially adventuresome—like skydiving or climbing Mt. Everest—if he knew death was imminent, he found instead that his deepest desire was to reconnect with the ordinary. So he moved back home for three months, spending time with his parents and puttering around the house and yard. Then he bicycled across the country for three months to visit each of his five siblings, sleeping at night under the stars in the backyards of people who let him pitch his tent on their property, often sharing a cup of coffee or tea with them over conversations in the evenings. He also cleaned out his bank account, sending anonymous monetary gifts to people he knew and loved. It was, he said, the first genuinely altruistic thing he had ever done in his life.

The hardest part of believing you're going to die, he said, is not being able to think about a future. How difficult it is to hear a piece of music and to imagine that you might never hear it again. Or to see something beautiful you want to show someone else and to think you will never get the chance. The loss of the future, he said, was the hardest part.

At the end of his bicycle sojourn, this young man returned to his parents' home just in time for Halloween—fully expecting not to wake up the day after. He had completely convinced himself he was going to die, and Halloween marked the end of the six months since he vowed to live until he died. When he did actually awake the next morning, he was overwhelmed by the enormous sense of life's giftedness. He was not dead; he was alive. "I was *reborn into ordinariness*," he said, "but what more could I ask for?" (emphasis added). And within his soul there was deep-rooted joy at the prospect of being able to regain a future lived in ordinary time.

As I listened, it dawned on me that what I most desire this Jubilee Year is to be reborn to the ordinary. I long for freedom and space from my overcommitted, anxiety-producing, run-about public life in which simply to "be" and to rediscover the simple pleasures that are all around me. I want to take morning walks, to read, to pray, to watch birds feed and deer graze, to plant flowers, to cook for the fun of it, to sit with my beloved spouse before dinner, drinking wine while reflecting on our respective days. I want to write notes to people I'm thinking of, to wrap care packages for my children in other places, to cook a meal for a person in need, and to volunteer for something I believe in.

Last week I saw a television special in which Paul McCartney was interviewed by his daughter about his life. Sir Paul recounted how, at one point after the Beatles had dissolved and he was depressed and uncertain about the future, he and his family simply "dropped out" of their fast-paced, notorious life for a season; moved to a small, remote farm in Scotland; and rediscovered the ordinary. It was obvious, as he and his daughter reminisced—about the time and about their life with their wife/mother Linda (who later died of breast cancer), and as they flashed pictures on the screen of themselves tromping through sheep pastures in knee boots or riding horseback through an open field—that this season of their family's life had been one of their happiest. It was ordinary time, imbued and infused with the holiness of life lived fully in community with nature and with those beloved.

I hunger for such ordinary time. Who knows when death will come to me, my husband, our children, our parents, our siblings? Whenever it comes, I don't want to feel cheated by its advent. I don't want to feel that I've missed "being"—and being with those I love. Instead, I would prefer to face death with the knowledge that I have lived each day fully in the presence of the ordinary—so that the ordinary becomes revelatory to me of the lovely, miraculous, extraordinary grace of its Creator and Sustainer.

So I'm going to get a book on trees so that I can enjoy by name the majestic trees in my new backyard; and a book on birds so that I can identify and greet the birds that come to the feeder. I'm going to plant flowers, talk to the deer who roam our yard, discover how to use fresh herbs in cooking, buy more jazz albums, learn how to entertain simply (so I can savor time with our guests rather than spending all my time frustrated in preparation), take swing dance lessons with my husband, light candles, listen to the rain on the roof, get to know the children in our church, and enjoy the company of newfound friends. I'm also going to email the transcript of yesterday's program to my daughter. She, who excels in living each day fully, would love it. I know.

Scripture Reading: Matthew 6:25–34

For Further Reflection
— If you were to be "reborn to the ordinary," what aspects of your life would you like to give up?
— What aspects would you like to attend to more closely?
— How might you incorporate more "being" and less "doing" into your daily life rhythms?

THE ORCHID PLANT

My husband and I laugh about our orchid plant. He says it would win a prize at a county fair for having the lushest, greenest, thickest leaves of all. He likens them—because of their thickness and texture—to portabella mushrooms. The only problem is, this plant never blooms.

The plant was a gift from dear friends who stayed with us several years ago. We were out of town for the last few days of their visit, and when we returned home a beautiful orchid was sitting on our dining room table as an expression of their thanks. Its delicate purple-pink blossoms delighted us for several weeks as it bloomed, and when the petals withered and died, I trusted more would soon appear. But in two years they never have.

For the first year of its life, my neglect hindered the well-being of this plant. Those were stressful years during which I treated the orchid with the same sort of benign neglect I treat the other plants in our household—giving it an occasional douse of water and trusting it would care for itself. When various little brown spikes started appearing at its base without blooming, I cut them off.

About a year ago, I met a florist at a party and told her about my plant. She looked appalled when I told her I had cut off the brown stems. "Those are the roots!" she said. Instead of a small dose of water several times a week, she encouraged me to give the orchid a thorough watering once a week—preferably on the same day—with tepid water. "When you get ready to water it, mix some orchid food in with warm water, and then pour it over the plant for about thirty seconds—as you hold the plant over the sink—until the medium around it is saturated. Let the excess drain off.

And then just let the plant sit in the sun until the next week when you water it again. If you do this," she promised, "it should start blooming in about six to eight weeks."

For the past year, I have faithfully heeded her advice, and with good results. This plant now has the lushest, thickest leaves of any orchid I have ever seen. And one of its roots is now quite lengthy, stretching out to meet the sun. But the plant has yet to bloom.

It occurred to me how much my orchid is a metaphor for my life during this Jubilee Year. For the first time in my life, I am basking in the sun and letting my starved soul be drenched in the warm and welcoming waters of rebirth and renewal. I have felt my roots growing longer, stretching out toward the sun that is life to me. I am back in touch with the basics I need for living—water, air, spirit, food— and I know that I am healthier than I was some months before I started this journey. My leaves—once a sickly pale green—are now lush and vibrant, a deep jade green. My survival is no more in question. I am strong, I am healthy, and I am once again fully alive.

But I also know, way down in the depths of my soul, that I haven't yet bloomed. Though I am beginning to tap into sources of creativity that have lain dormant for far too many years, I have yet to produce those delicate blossoms that delight the heart and fill the soul with joy. I have yet to discover the fullness of all that God intends for me to become.

Just as it takes many months to stifle beauty and creativity in a growing plant or person, so too, it takes many months to restore and resurrect them. The leaves are the first sure sign of renewed health and vitality. But leaves alone are not enough. God wants us to blossom and flourish.

In John's Gospel, Jesus is aware that his disciples are heading for tough times. He will soon be leaving them, and he knows that they will become disheartened and discouraged and spent. So he tells them what they must do to keep their lives healthy and strong. "Abide in me," he says, "as I abide in you. Just as the branch cannot bear fruit by itself unless it abides in the vine, neither can you unless you abide in me. I am the vine, you are the branches. Those who abide in me and I in them bear much fruit, because apart from me you can do nothing" (John 15:4–5).

Often when we get pushed and stressed in life, the first thing we let go are those very spiritual practices that ground us in God and make us healthy, productive human beings. Worship becomes sporadic; we have little time for prayer; our Bibles collect dust on our shelves. Ironically, though we may think we are letting go of those parts of our lives that are not as "productive" as others, we are actually cutting off our own roots. We are separating ourselves from the one true Vine that can nurture and nourish us and make us bloom.

"Abide in me . . ." Jesus says, "so that my joy may be in you, and that your joy may be complete" (John 15: 4a, 11b).

Scripture Reading: John 15:1–11

For Further Reflection
— Using the image of an orchid, how would you assess the state of your own spiritual health these days? Are your leaves glossy and strong or withering and pale? Are you blossoming or simply putting forth abundant foliage? Are your roots getting that which they need to sustain and nourish them? Or are you, by neglect, cutting them off from their source of health and life?
— What new practices might you need to undertake to nourish that most precious of plants—your soul and spirit?

A RAINBOW ON MY FOOT

A crazy thing happened to me last Sunday morning. I was standing in the shower, getting ready to go to church, when I looked down and behold there was a rainbow across my foot. No, I'm not speaking metaphorically here. I'm speaking literally. The shower stall—with its clear glass door—stands right across from a window in our small bathroom, and somehow the sun was refracted through both sets of glass so as to create a rainbow on my right foot. All I had to do was move my foot an inch or so in the right direction, and the rainbow literally formed an arch across my entire foot.

The fact that this bow appeared on my *right* foot is important, because just the day before I had been looking at that particular foot in a shoe store mirror, bemoaning its disfigured state. I used to have feet that matched pretty well, but I don't any longer. Ever since I had surgery on my right ankle some months ago, my right foot has been a lot larger than my left. Finding shoes that fit both feet now is nigh unto impossible. And the right ankle always looks swollen—like my arthritic eighty-year-old grandmother's ankles always looked. Add to that reality the numerous visible, broken, and varicose veins in that ankle, and you've got an ugly sight. An old foot on a woman who considers herself, at age fifty, still young.

But here I was—on a Sunday morning in the Easter season—standing in the shower, the water cascading over my body, with a rainbow on my foot! I don't quite know what to make of it, but it does remind me of two sermons I've heard.

The first is actually a sermon I preached a number

of years ago to a group of pastors. In it I contrasted the images that were found in two of the biblical lectionary readings for the day in order to talk about the joys and the tribulations of ministry. In the first reading from Isaiah 52, the prophet celebrates the feet of messengers who bring the good news of God's peace, calling them "beautiful." I used this text to evoke memories of times in ministry when the proclamation of good news has been celebrated and received in joy and thanksgiving and gratitude by parishioners. Times when people have come out the door after worship and said to their pastor, "My, your feet are beautiful!"

In the text from Galatians 4, on the other hand, the apostle Paul is angry and frustrated by his congregation's lack of receptivity to the gospel he proclaims. He tells them he is having "labor pains" because they refuse to allow Christ to be born within them. Indeed, they are resisting this birth—and their own rebirth—so much that the apostle is unable to deliver the gospel in their midst.

Like the prophets of old, ministers today can also encounter strenuous resistance to the good news of God's coming reign of justice and righteousness and peace—especially when the inauguration of that reign will be costly to the hearers. So preachers also know what it is like to stand at the door after church and have their beloved congregants greet them, not with praise for their beautiful feet, but with anger over their prophetic witness.

The second sermon is one I heard preached by a favorite pastor of mine during the Vietnam War. At a time when our nation desperately longed for an all-too-elusive peace, this pastor/prophet used the Genesis 9 text about Noah and the flood to remind us of God's promise to us through the rainbow. By taking a common weapon of war, the bow, and bending it and placing it in the sky, God has given us a multicolored promise that, one day, all weapons of war will be turned into plowshares, spears changed into pruning hooks, and nations will not study war any more (see Isa. 2:4). One day God will redeem all death—including those caused by war—and shall bring to birth out of this world's wickedness a new reign of life, refracted in light and hope.

What does all this have to do with my foot? Frankly, I'm not altogether sure I know. But I do have an inkling or two.

A pastoral counselor I know says that whenever we have a serious ache in a body part it is also symbolic of something else going on in our lives. She visited me right after I first broke my ankle and laid this pearl of wisdom on me right after hearing about how difficult my vocational life had been in recent months. When I heard it, I laughed out loud. "And what," I asked incredulously, "does my broken ankle have to do with anything that has been going on in my life in recent years?" Without missing a beat she replied, "Do you have any idea how many times you have used language with me today that has to do with feet and standing? Time and again you have said. 'I had to leave. I didn't have a choice. There was simply no place left where I could safely stand.' Is it any wonder that it is your ankle that has been broken?"

I don't know what it means to have a rainbow appear across my foot on a Sunday morning. But I'll take it as a sign of promise: Promise of a coming day in which God's justice will reign so that all people—even those who, like the martyrs, bear in their bodies the brokenness of this world's unjust powers—have a place where they can safely and securely stand. Promise of a coming time when the labor pains of breached births give way to the glorious liberty of the children of God. And promise of a day in which God will take even the most bruised and swollen and misshapen of feet and, through redemptive power, turn them into something beautiful—absolutely beautiful.

Scripture Reading: Genesis 9:8–17; Isaiah 52:7–10

For Further Reflection
— Do you currently have a physical ailment or pain that might be symbolic of something larger going on in your life? If so, what is it, and what does it signify for you?
— Have you ever heard a messenger of God's peace speak something so hopeful and so profound that you thought his or her feet were beautiful? Reflect on that messenger and what it was about the message that made it so life-giving for you.
— What does the image of the rainbow—with its promise of God's peace—mean to you in your current life situation?

THE GREENING OF LIFE

Spring always comes late in the Northeast, or so it seems to me. I grew up in coastal North Carolina where the weather was so mild that people sometimes played golf in January. Winter never lasted long enough for me there, and spring—beautiful though it was—often seemed but a brief interlude on the way to summer. By May the days had turned hot and muggy, and by June the heat was unbearable.

Spring in the Northeast is different. It comes late, lasts longer, and is always, always welcome. The trees stand stoic and bare against the bleak landscape for months upon end, and just when you think you cannot bear winter another day, buds begin making their appearance. When the dogwoods finally flower, their blossoms are an absolute marvel. "How did this happen?" you ask yourself. "Just last week there were only buds on this tree."

The grass, too, seems to green instantly. My brother Jim, who lives in Detroit, says the grass always turns green at once in the North—and on a particular day of the year. This year, he announced, it was the second Tuesday in April. (Funny, that's the day it turned green in New Jersey, too.)

And when, at last, the hardwood trees—the last holdouts—finally begin to bear their new spring-green coats (I always liken the color to the yellow-green color in the Crayola 64 box) you think to yourself, "Hooray! I've actually made it through another winter. Life is definitely greening up. Spring, at long last, has arrived."

These days, my sun-porch views abound with signs of spring. The cardinal couple is back at the feeder each morning, returned from their winter sojourn to a mysterious, unknown winter home. They huddle together, pecking away at their breakfast on the green plastic deck of the feeder, his vibrant red feathers against her muted brown and red, yin and yang personified. I find myself wondering whether they, like geese, mate for life.

The deer are also coming closer than they did in winter, roaming right past the porch to the front yard to feast on the new tree leaves and the tender shoots of grass that have been denied them too long. Several appear to be "great with child," and it won't be long until their spotted fawns will roam the yard with them.

From the upstairs bedroom window I see a large, red-headed, black-and-white checked woodpecker going to town on a dead tree at the end of the woods, in search of insects. (How in the world woodpeckers avoid having their brains scrambled in their rat-a-tat quest for food is beyond me.) Huge and determined and vibrant in his bright spring jacket and hat, he stands—reminiscent of children in their Easter finery—silhouetted against the brown, lifeless color of the log.

Yesterday I was so inspired by this outbreak of spring that I spent the entire afternoon in the lawn and garden section of a local store, trying to decide which colors of flowers to plant in the multiple baskets I want to hang around the yard this year (hopefully just out of reach of the deer). I settled on purple and white and salmon petunias for the planters, bought matching baskets with pink begonias to hang from the deck, a purple and pink fuchsia for hanging under the branches of the backyard oak tree, and then—on a whim—added a gardenia bush for the sunporch, its white flowers and glossy deep-green leaves a sweet-smelling reminder of my southern heritage. I never smell a gardenia that I don't think of my southern grandmothers—both of whom loved them.

I used to think of buying flowers as a luxury. And in the grand scheme of things, they certainly rank behind food and shelter and other basics we need for physical survival. But when it comes to the survival of the spirit, I find that flowers are essential. Remember that poem about buying hyacinths when you have run out of money?

> If of thy mortal goods thou art bereft,
> and from thy slender store
> Two loaves alone to thee are left,
> Sell one, and with the dole
> Buy Hyacinths to feed thy Soul.*

I think of it often — especially on grocery shopping days when my first stop is to pick out a fresh bouquet of flowers for the dining room table. "Why is it," I think to myself, "that I spent so many years of my life thinking flowers were only for company?"

I don't know the answer to that question. But I do know that I have become, in this my Jubilee Year, a lavish lover of the greening of life. I need to grow things, and I need to be around growing things, in order to be most fully alive myself. I am intimately connected with Mother Earth, and when she blossoms, so do I.

Last night, as I prepared our evening meal, I couldn't help humming. Spring is back. Life is turning green again. And like the flowers in the hanging baskets on my deck, my joy is spilling over at its return.

Scripture Reading: Song of Solomon 2:8–15

---

*This poem is frequently attributed to the thirteenth-century Persian Sufi poet Moslih Eddin Saadi (Sa'di), who wrote a book of poems titled *Gulliston* [The Rose Garden].

For Further Reflection
— What do you love about springtime in your part of the world?
— What are the sure signs to you that spring is on its way?
— The poet in Song of Solomon revels in the joys of the spring season. What does it mean to you that God delights in the physicality of the natural world?

A DEER IN HEADLIGHTS

These days I find myself seeking out the company of other Jubilee women. Yesterday I had lunch with one. She's not fifty yet, but I think she hit her Jubilee stride a few years early. And oh, does it become her!

Adele, a professor in an academic institution, was diagnosed several years ago as having chronic fatigue syndrome. Forced to learn in her early forties to live with ongoing physical limitations, she revamped her entire lifestyle, weeding out the nonessentials in her life and carefully preserving her limited energies for those things most important to her. To do so, of course, is not a once-and-for-all proposition. She constantly has to guard against the pressures our hyper-achieving culture places on her to take on yet one more commitment.

Yesterday she told me about an all-too-familiar incident that happened last week when her academic dean caught her in the hallway and announced (out of the blue), "Adele, I've assigned you to meet regularly with a formation group of students this semester."

"Pardon me," Adele responded. "Since when do we not discuss these things first?"

"This is the discussion," the dean replied.

So Adele quickly thought through her carefully balanced schedule, identified one place where she could possibly cut back on other commitments, and agreed to take it on. But the reality was that it was a *fait accompli* before she even responded. No real "discussion" was ever intended.

"He caught me like a deer in headlights," she said. "And I don't want that to happen again."

I thought, as she spoke, of how often I and others of my acquaintance—especially other working women—have been caught like a deer in headlights. Some decision—usually made behind closed doors by an inner circle of men in power—is pronounced in a moment when we least expect it, rendering us dazed, immobile, and too immediately taken aback to say much of anything. All of a sudden we find that our lives have been upended by decisions we had no part in making.

Adele's solution to this problem (one she laughingly shared with me) is that she has been rehearsing, over and over again with her husband, the response she will make the next time this happens. "I'll check my calendar and get back with you," she'll say to her dean. And if he insists that it is a done deal, she will again assert, even more boldly, "I'll check my calendar and get back with you," as she walks away. Thus she will claim her own power and authority as a decision maker.

I wish we women didn't have to rehearse for such moments in our lives. I wish we didn't have to be so vigilant in protecting our precious, limited energies from those who would squander and spend them as if they did not belong to us. But all too often, I fear we do.

Unless, that is, we can find a space in which to graze and frolic and live out our vocations where the hunters do not roam the fields with guns cocked and lights blazing. That is my heart's desire. It seems also to be the desire of the psalmists of old, who speak with longing and gratitude of a God who leads vulnerable creatures to green pastures and ever-flowing streams and who protects them from the traps and snares of evildoers who would prey on their vulnerability.

I am deeply grateful these days for the joy and freedom of this Jubilee existence. No hunters. No guns. No headlights. I can't help but wonder, though: in the world of here-and-now institutions, do such spaces actually exist? Can deer actually find safe pasture for grazing this side of heaven?

Scripture Reading: Psalm 42

For Further Reflection
— Have you ever been caught in a situation where you felt like a deer in headlights? How did you respond?
— How do you wish you had responded?
— What might you do next time to prevent your power and authority from being usurped?

HOUSEWORK

I am of the generation that often considered housework —
because of its traditional assignment to women — demean-
ing, an activity to be avoided if at all possible. I grew up
a dutiful daughter — doing assigned chores around the
house — and also insisted that both my children do them.
I polished furniture, ironed, took out the garbage, and
cleaned bathtubs and toilets. I was supposed to keep my
room clean as well, but as a teenager, I had the messiest
room in the house. Indeed, I was quite adept at keeping
one side of my double bed piled high with clothes and
books while I slept in the other half!

When I reached adulthood and lived on my own, I did
the minimal amount needed to keep a house respectable.
I was never obsessive about a clean house, though. It was
only when floors and sinks got really dirty — that I deemed
it necessary to clean. And then it was a last resort. I always
had more important things to do.

After I married, my husband, Alfred, and I eventually
worked out a division of labor in the household that typ-
ically meant (in our early years) that he took care of the
yard and did a few household chores, and I did the rest.
Neighbors in our first parish used to laugh at my spouse's
multitasking abilities. For it was typical of Al to cut the
grass with our infant daughter, Leonora, in a pack on his
back, our black Labrador retriever tied to a leash (so he
could walk the dog as he mowed the lawn), while sermon
ideas percolated in his brain.

What I remember from those early years is that, in my
still delusional state of thinking I could do everything at

once, I tried hard to do just that. Even after our second child was born and we were pastors of four churches, I still refused to purchase disposable diapers (environmentally unsound), use a laundry service (too expensive), or hire anyone to clean our house (didn't want the pastors to appear to be living "above" our parishioners). Instead, I have vivid memories of hanging cloth diapers on the line in weather so cold that they froze the minute they were hung, of drying racks set up in the den near the woodstove on snowy days, and of floors that were never clean for more than two minutes.

During this, my Jubilee Year, I am coming to see housework differently. Like monks who take on daily chores—baking bread or gardening or washing dishes—as a part of their spiritual discipline, I see the work I do in making our house a cleaner and more presentable home as being a part of my spiritual discipline. Life seems more in balance when I am not simply living life as a scholar (reading, writing, thinking, speaking) but also as a manual laborer, working with my hands and my back to complete the basic tasks needed to keep our house clean, our clothes washed and folded. It is satisfying to see the bathrooms sparkle and to walk across a newly mopped floor (though the mopping task is still the one I dislike the most). It is good to do work in which I can see immediate results for a change—even if they are fleeting.

But I am also aware that this work is still not highly valued, that women still do most of it, and that many men don't have a clue how time-consuming or wearying it really is. There is something fundamentally wrong about a world in which some labor is honored while other labor is considered "menial."

A friend of mine says that after a very difficult period in her own life as an academic, it was the mindless routine of doing daily household chores that eventually helped to restore her soul and spirit, and gave her back her imagination, creativity, and zest for life. She is writing and dreaming and teaching again—and also doing housework as a part of her ongoing spiritual discipline. It was, for her, a part of "letting the ground lie fallow," letting her mind rest so that it could grow fertile and productive again.

Frankly, I think there's wisdom in this routine—not just for a season but for a lifetime. In more recent years, my husband has taken on more household chores (including, God bless him, the mopping), and I have begun helping more with the yard. We have a rhythm that works for us, and we enjoy doing tasks together and in a manner that seems fairer and more equitable to us both.

Yet the other (perhaps more formidable) challenge is this: How do we value and reclaim as significant and worthwhile work that the world so regularly devalues and demeans? How do we make "holy" that which the world has so regularly profaned?

In the parable of the Lost Coin in Luke's Gospel, Jesus likens the realm of God's reign to a woman who, when she loses a coin of value, searches her whole house until she finds it. She sweeps and cleans and searches diligently until at last she finds her coin, and then she calls her friends and neighbors to come and have a party with her because her precious coin has been found. Her housework actually becomes for her a quest for the Holy—which she finds, not outside her ordinary vocational sphere, but within it.

This parable is sandwiched between the parable of the shepherd who leaves ninety-nine sheep in order to search for one lost sheep (Luke 15:3–7), and the parable of the father who rushes out to welcome his lost son home (Luke 15:11–32)—as if to suggest that whether our work is keeping sheep or cleaning houses or parenting, there is something of God within it—if only we have the perseverance to look for it, and eyes to recognize it when we find it.

Scripture Reading: Luke 15:8–10

For Further Reflection
— Where do you glimpse signs of the Holy in the ordinary work or activities of your life?
— How might that work space become less drudgery and duty for you, and more hallowed ground, where God might be uncovered at any minute?

IN PRAISE OF LYDIA

The business manager at our church told me recently that she aspires to become the Lydia of our congregation. She sees Lydia as a person who excelled in extending hospitality to others, and she believes her calling is to be one who extends that same sort of gracious, welcoming hospitality to all who come through our doors.

The truth of the matter is: this woman already *is* Lydia. And through her I see Lydia anew. She is capable and efficient in running the business of our church—personnel, budgets, hiring, overseeing—just as Lydia must have been capable in running her fabric-dyeing business. But our business manager is so much more than that. She is also gracious, welcoming, encouraging, supportive, and kind. She remembers birthdays with thoughtful gifts or cards, writes notes of appreciation to those who have worked hard, buys flowers for those who direct church plays or musicals, welcomes strangers who wander into our church building, sits many Sunday mornings with a physically challenged member of the congregation who needs assistance receiving Communion, deals tactfully with church volunteers, and has—on more than one occasion—eased my own anxieties and fears when a task I had taken on seemed too huge or daunting.

Recently, we invited the staff of our new church to our home for a pot-luck Christmas lunch. "Lydia" sent out the invitations to this party. I was pleased that she included not only the program staff (pastors, musicians, educators) but also the secretaries, sextons, and others who work behind the scenes to make our church an efficient and welcoming environment for all. When it came time for the gift exchange, the number of gifts exactly matched the number of guests, although I knew that at least one guest had not brought a gift. Who else, I thought, but Lydia?

One of the many things I love about our Lydia is that she brings the best of two worlds together in her own being. She is efficient *and* gracious; she attends closely to budgets *and* somehow manages to multiply loaves and fishes; she is boss *and* friend, supervisor *and* shepherd.

Our world has not always valued Lydias, or even thought their calling worthy. For years church women were handmaids of male church leaders who took their labor-intensive acts of hospitality for granted while also denying women an equal voice in running the business of the church. One woman recently told me that when she left the patriarchal world of corporate business and began volunteering more at her church, she soon found herself gravitate toward the kitchen and the company of women, because at church meetings she encountered the same devaluing of her voice that she had encountered in the business world. "I chose to be in the kitchen," she said, "because there I didn't have to deal with the same patriarchal crap all over again."

It is easy for those of us in leadership positions — whether male or female — to buy into a dichotomizing model of administration that devalues the hospitality of the Lydias of this world or that deems small acts of kindness toward those who work with and for us as less important than efficiency and budget crunching. Yet I also sense that the new wave of leadership in the future — for both women and men — will be the Lydia way.

A friend called this week to say his company has been downsized, and he has quit his job. Although he greatly enjoyed the working relationships with coworkers in the office he managed, he increasingly found himself in the untenable position of having to rank order his employees on the basis of productivity alone, with no consideration given to the personal issues in their lives that affected their job performance. "How do I let that employee and friend go whose work has suffered this quarter because his child has leukemia? I can't do it anymore. Next time around, I'm looking for a non-management job—even if it requires a salary cut." The irony, of course, is that he is exactly the kind of manager the world most needs.

To be a Lydia may not make good business sense, but it certainly makes good human sense—and good gospel sense.

Scripture Reading: Acts 16:11–15, 35–40

For Further Reflection
— Think of a person you know who is like Lydia. What are the traits that make her or him so? How might you express your gratitude to this person for being such a witness in your life?
— Reflect on your own life. What are the traits of Lydia that you would most like to emulate? Are there traits you would want to avoid?
— How do you hold on to the best traits of Lydia without, in the process, giving yourself away?

TURKEY ROOST

Last evening, as my husband and I were eating dinner, we watched a very large, wild turkey hen—whom we had recently sighted roaming our yard with her five chicks trailing behind her—lift her giant wings and fly up into the high branches of an oak tree to make her perch for the night. Astonished, since the only turkeys I had previously seen were the domesticated type who were almost rooted to the ground, we marveled at her ability to lift herself at all, much less to soar to a place of safety and rest. Patiently, she sat on the tree branch as each of her chicks in turn paced the ground below for a while and then dared to lift its own less-developed wings and follow her in the flight toward safety. As we looked upward into the tree, we could see all six of them, spreading out onto the branches of that tree and adjoining trees, going higher and higher until they were totally camouflaged from all predators that would seek them out in the cover of night.

How much like God the mother turkey hen is! She doesn't push, she doesn't shove, she doesn't force. She just shows us the way, goes there before us to prepare a place, and then encourages us to follow—trusting that we, like she, will be born up on our seemingly too-small-for-our-bodies wings to a place of safety and rest.

I thought of the turkeys again as I watched the late news, with its coverage of all the ways in which people are frantically trying to secure themselves. In the wake of the World Trade Center attacks, and in the face of imminent war, people are rushing out to army surplus stores to purchase gas masks and stock up on antibiotics to "secure" themselves against enemy predators whose chemical or biological weapons might attack under cover of night. One woman purchased eighteen gas masks, one for each of her family members. Yet when a reporter interviewed a researcher at the Center for Disease Control, he basically said such efforts are futile. Unless we wear gas masks twenty-four hours a day, seven days a week, there is no guarantee that we will be protected from an invisible disease when it becomes airborne. And unless we have just the right antibiotic on hand, our medicine will render us helpless in the face of whatever particular strain of the disease we might contract.

Our real safety, our true security, lies elsewhere: in a God who provides shelter for us even in the darkest of nights and in a hope that defies the odds in its power to lift us skyward at a time when the world around us seems to be spiraling downward into war. It is not cheap escapism I envision here. Rather, it is a larger protective Mother God, whose will it is that not a one of her children should perish.

This morning, in the predawn light, I wandered out into my backyard to see if I could glimpse those large birds roosting in our backyard tree. I couldn't see them; they were invisible through the canopy of leaves. But I could hear them, clucking to one another as they awoke to behold a new dawn. By the time the sun had fully risen, they were long gone, off roaming the woods behind us for another day of food gathering and grand adventure.

Scripture Reading: Psalm 18:1–19

For Further Reflection
The psalmist proclaims that God is our rock, our fortress, our refuge, and our deliverer. Yet it is often hard for us humans to trust in that promise. Instead we spend an

enormous amount of energy and resources trying to secure ourselves and those we love.

— What does it mean to you to trust that God, like the mother turkey hen, has prepared a place for you to roost in safety?
— Where have you previously witnessed God's deliverance and protection in your life and the lives of those you love?
— What would it take for you to be willing to test your own fledgling wings and fly?

WRESTLING WITH WAR

For most of my adult life, I have been a closet pacifist. This is, in large part, because, ever since the Vietnam War, I really haven't had to declare myself one way or the other.

All of this changed, of course, on September 11, 2001. In a sermon I preached at our church some months after the attack, I poked my head out of the closet at least, expressing my admiration for Harry Emerson Fosdick, the famous first pastor of The Riverside Church in New York, who preached pacifism throughout World War II. I talked about how it was Fosdick's own pastoral involvement with troops on the front lines in World War I that led him to embrace his pacifist stance, even as he openly welcomed service men and women to worship at Riverside throughout WWII and opened the sanctuary on Sunday afternoons for the Navy Midshipmen's Training School services of worship. The major point I was making is that shepherding the flock of Christ involves not only tending sheep but also fending off wolves (including our own warring madness), but the side point was also clear: I admire Fosdick and the courage he exhibited in being a pacifist during WWII.

After the service, a parishioner I'll call Daniel, a German immigrant who is a member of our congregation, approached me — his face deeply troubled. He asked how I could express admiration for a man who was a pacifist in World War II? If it weren't for America's involvement in WWII, Germany might still be ruled by Hitler's tyranny. Did I not understand how critical America's involvement in that war was for the well-being of the whole world?

I wanted to shrug off Daniel's objections to my sermon,

but his face still haunts me—a face with eyes that have seen too much, like the eyes of those who witnessed the holocaust of a burning building and people leaping out of the windows.

I have thought of Daniel this week as I have been reading Denise Giardina's gripping novel, *Saints and Villains*, a fictional account of the life of the German pastor and theologian Dietrich Bonhoeffer. The novel tells the story of Bonhoeffer's ethical and human struggles with a Christian response to war in light of the terror of Hitler's rule and of his own ultimate decision to participate in a plot to assassinate and overthrow Hitler.

In one pivotal scene in the novel—when Bonhoeffer is still refusing to participate in the plot against Hitler advocated by his father and brother yet is also endangering Jewish in-laws in the family by his outspokenness against Hitler's regime—his brother-in-law Karl-Friedrich, confronts him: "you don't want your hands dirty? For the sake of your religious convictions, I suppose," Karl-Friedrich laughed. "You Christians. You'll make sure you don't endanger the salvation of your precious souls, but you don't mind if someone else does the dirty work for you. Give me an atheist any day."*

Sometimes I wonder if this is me, sitting on the sidelines as we engage in a war in Afghanistan—secretly rejoicing that the women might have a chance of being freed from patriarchy, secretly giving thanks for the food and aid that might now get through to refugees, secretly hoping that Osama Bin Laden would be brought to a swift and sure justice—all the while leaving the dirty work to others as I claim the higher moral ground.

I'm having to rethink my closet pacifism—just as

*Denise Giardina, *Saints and Villains* (New York: Fawcett Books, The Ballantine Publishing Group, 1998), 235.

Bonhoeffer did—and I don't like it. Jesus was a pacifist. I'm sure of it. But am I? Really? Somehow it's a lot harder at this age and stage of life to imagine myself watching my children—or the world's children, for that matter—being viciously slaughtered and doing nothing, even if the only thing that would stop the slaughter were a violent act.

Living with yourself *either* way would be hell—no question about it. Both Bonhoeffer and Fosdick are heroes in that respect. Neither, given his time and place of ministry, chose an easy path.

But in the final analysis, it's not all about courage, as admirable as courage is. The choice is about faithfulness to God and about discerning the faithful path to follow in times when justice and peace are at war.

By choosing the cross instead of the warring ways of the Zealots, did Jesus trade away justice for peace? Supposedly not. But that's the point at which many of us Christians still wrestle and wrestle mightily. Do we honestly believe—as Jesus taught—that justice ultimately comes only through suffering, nonviolent love—even of our enemies? And if so, are we willing to come out of the closet and boldly stake our claim?

Scripture Reading: Matthew 5:43–48

For Further Reflection
— How has your faith influenced your belief about war?
— Do you think Jesus was a pacifist? Why or why not?
— Do you find yourself agreeing more with the path taken by Fosdick or with the path taken by Bonhoeffer, and why?

BATTLING ILLNESS

(WRITTEN AT AGES 51–52, 61)

INTRODUCTION TO THIS SECTION

In January of 2003, only a few weeks after I had completed my "Year of Jubilee" and begun a new job at a large church in New York City, I was diagnosed with breast cancer. The diagnosis came unexpectedly during a routine mammogram.

At first, I was bewildered by the diagnosis. There was no history of breast cancer in my family, and I had been, on the whole, diligent about getting annual mammograms. (I had, however, missed having a mammogram the previous year.) More puzzling to me was the fact that I had just enjoyed the most relaxed and stress-free year of my adult life: my Year of Jubilee. "How could this be happening NOW?" I asked my husband. He gently replied that it takes a long time for cancer to show itself in a lump, and that perhaps it was the stress of the prior years—not the rest of the immediate past year—that had given me cancer. I am convinced he was right.

So 2003 became the year when I battled Stage 2 breast cancer. I had a lumpectomy, in which it was revealed that five of the eleven lymph nodes in my right breast area were also infected. I then underwent chemotherapy and radiation treatments.

The church where I worked could not have been more supportive. I was able to keep working my part-time job, and indeed, the prayers and support of the staff and members of that wonderful congregation (Fifth Avenue Presbyterian Church in New York City) were a critical part of my healing process. I was also blessed to have amazingly supportive family and friends and excellent medical personnel—including Dr. Ellen Early (my personal cancer warrior) of the Carol Simon Cancer Center in Morris-town, New Jersey.

I wrote most of the meditations that follow during that year. (The exceptions are duly noted.) While I know that they are somewhat dated—treatments for cancer are con-stantly being improved—I share them because I think that certain spiritual and existential themes carry through—whatever illness a person is facing. I also share them because my year with cancer proved to be both the worst of times and the best of times. The worst of times part is obvious. But the best of times came from a renewed reli-ance on God and a strong sense that I had never walked more closely with God than I did during that year of ill-ness. The title of John Robert McFarland's book, which a friend gave me that year, resonated with me deeply: *Now That I Have Cancer, I Am Whole*.

I have now been cancer free for over a dozen years, and I am deeply grateful for each day of life I enjoy. But in the intervening years, I have watched all too many people I know and love face their own battles with cancer, some of them having lost their lives to it. My prayer is that these meditations will especially benefit those who are battling illness and those who care for them.

THE SUN STILL RISES

In the first few weeks following my diagnosis and surgery for breast cancer, I have found that I simply cannot tolerate bad news . . . any bad news. Whether it is local bad news (a multicar accident on a nearby highway), national news (school shootings or terrorist attacks), or international news (reports of war and starvation), I have a very low tolerance for bad news. It is as if my pain threshold has plummeted to rock bottom, so that any sadness, any pain, any suffering threatens to overwhelm and immobilize me. My soul and body cry out: "No more! We've got all that we can handle right now." I am earnestly trying to listen to them and to protect them.

Since I have always been one of those people who felt I could deal with anything—as long as it was out in the open—my own defense against bad news surprises me. An ostrich mentality has never been a hallmark of my personality! But this inner knowledge that I simply cannot bear any more pain has also given me new empathy and understanding for others who have suffered far worse tragedies in their lives than I—those who have posted invisible signs on the doors of their hearts that read, "Quarantined. No Bad News Allowed."

What I have found I most needed in recent weeks— probably more than at any other time in my life—are signs of hope. Anything that speaks of hope and life and light are welcome to me. Any harbinger of terror or death or pain is unwelcome.

That is why, when friends and relatives and colleagues sent flowers to my home in the week following my surgery, I welcomed each bouquet as if it were a personal gift from my Creator, bringing with it the promise of beauty and life and spring. I especially loved the tulips friends in Atlanta and Denver sent, and the amazing basket that arrived from my college roommate—full of baby jonquils and irises and crocus and narcissus. The card read, "Spring is on the way."

That is why I also spend so much time staring out the window at the birds that flock to our feeder. If God so cares for the sparrows and the lilies, then surely God also cares for me.

And that is why my early morning ritual of watching the sunrise has become critical to my healing. I need to know that the sun still rises. I need to see it happen. For with the rising of the sun comes also the promise that this world is in God's hands, that the one who watches over us neither slumbers nor sleeps, and that "from the rising of the sun to its setting," our lives are in God's hands.

My sunrise ritual is simple but proves to be enormously healing for me. I try to arrive at my sunporch just before dawn actually breaks. In the darkness, I turn up the heat (I love to hear the water gurgle through the steam heating pipes!) as I light the seven candles that are scattered around the room—many of them loving gifts from friends and family. One piece of music that has most deeply spoken to me in recent weeks—often like the Holy Spirit, praying for me with "sighs too deep for words"—is a choral work by contemporary Lutheran composer Morten Lauridsen called *Lux Aeterna*. In that work—performed in Latin so that the words flow through me but do not consume my attention—Lauridsen actually emulates the rising of the sun through his use of notes and musical intervals. To watch the sunrise between the bare winter trees of our backyard, to see the sky change from deep purple to deep blue and pink while listening to Lauridsen's ethereal music in the soft-scented glow of candlelight, is to encounter the Holy Other in all Its mystery and wonder. It is the time in my day when I most palpably feel the presence of God and when I also most deeply sense that my own weary soul and sick body can indeed rest in the arms of an infinitely loving embrace.

A longtime pastor friend—who also happens to be one of the most spiritual people I know—recently wrote that when his sister-in-law was undergoing her battle with lung cancer, she made a conscious decision during her times of treatment not to allow anything toxic (like news of war or violence) to intrude into her healing process. "She signs each of her letters to us, her groupies," he says, "with these encouraging words: 'The Sky is Still Blue.'"

I think I'll start signing my own letters, "The Sun Still Rises!" For when I watch the light of dawn break forth anew each morning, I also know—in the deepest core of my being—that God is God, that God's will for this world is for light and warmth and healing, and that the One who took on human flesh in all its crippling brokenness and pain will surely also embrace and encircle my brokenness with His own redemptive body.

Scripture Reading: Psalm 113:1–4

Prayer
O light born of light,
Jesus, the redeemer of the world,
mercifully deem worthy and accept
the praises and prayers of your supplicants.
You who once deigned to be clothed in flesh
for the sake of the lost one,
grant us to be made members
of your holy body.*

*This is David Wyatt's English translation of the ancient Latin version of Lauridsen's *O Nata Lux* ("O Light Born of Light") taken from Lauridsen's choral work *Lux Aeterna*.

NO ENERGY FOR ANGER

One of the things cancer has changed about me is that I have a lot less energy for anger than I used to have. The first challenge for my anger-adjustment attitude came a few days after I returned home from the hospital, having just endured a lumpectomy and the removal of many of the lymph nodes in my right arm. A crew of repairmen had chosen this unfortunate timing to install a new stove and microwave, replacing the ones I had accidentally burned in a kitchen fire during the Christmas holidays. I was delighted with the prospect of a working stove and microwave—especially given that my mother had just arrived from North Carolina to help care for us, and church members were arriving with food that we had no means to heat. But the presence of all those repairmen in my home, when I was feeling sick and tired and wanted only peace and quiet, was a trial. I had no energy to oversee the project, so I steered clear of it altogether until one of the workmen announced that the new units were installed and were in working order.

It was then that I discovered that the stove and microwave that had just been installed were black, while all my other kitchen appliances were white. When I expressed my dismay, the workers told me that I had a choice: I could either wait a week for them to order and install new white appliances (during which time I would have no appliances to use), or I could live with the black ones. Between the proverbial rock and hard place, I told them to leave the black ones installed.

But the anger gnawed at me. Why had I never been consulted about what color kitchen appliances I wanted in the first place? Why had the kitchen store manager assumed I wanted black and never asked me? Why had the project contractor not checked up on these details himself?

About a week later, when I was beginning to feel better, I made some phone calls and ended up even more frustrated. The kitchen store manager admitted he should have asked, but he swore to me that the former stove and microwave he had removed from my home were black (as if I, who had cooked in them for years, wouldn't know their color!) The contractor, who knew he was ultimately responsible, kept apologizing and muttering about how this was good reason for him never to do kitchen work again—but offered little real tangible help except a slight reduction in the cost.

Finally it occurred to me that the real decision-making power here was mine. I could either continue to fight for matching appliances—demanding the justice I knew I was rightfully due—or I could just let it all go. I could live with the mixed appliances in my kitchen.

If truth be told, when justice is at stake, I'm not one to lay down my anger easily. For me—and I suspect, for many of us—anger is the fuel that feeds our righteous rage and indignation and leads us from apathy to action. I've long appreciated the fact that one of Jesus' very first acts of compassion in John's Gospel is to drive out the money changers in the temple, who were robbing God's poor and oppressed people of their livelihood. This anger of Jesus is a "holy rage"—one that we too should emulate.

But let's face it. There is holy rage, and there is the other kind. My kitchen anger was definitely of the other ilk. It had more to do with my personal aesthetic preferences than with serving or saving the world. It was also the kind of rage, I ultimately realized, that could sap me of my precious healing energy if I continued to feed it and let it smolder.

So I decided to let it go. I paid my contractor his slightly reduced fee and thanked him for his efforts. I told him that while I knew the stove removed from my house was not black, I could live with this one. And I assured him that I would not hold this mistake against him in the future.

In the course of our daily lives, many of us are faced with similar decisions on a regular basis. What do we do about the car that has just passed all the rest of the cars behind us on the shoulder and now wants to squeeze in front of our car at the last minute? What do we do about the person at work who promised to do something but failed to execute that promise, leaving us to carry a heavier load? What attitude do we take when we try to work out a solution to a problem by phone, only to be put on hold countless times, wasting our precious time and energy?

When Maya Angelou was interviewed on her seventy-fourth birthday by Oprah Winfrey, she is said to have offered these words of wisdom:

> I've learned that no matter what happens, or how bad it seems today, life does go on and it will be better tomorrow. I've learned that you can tell a lot about a person by the way he/she handles these three things: a rainy day, lost luggage, and tangled Christmas tree lights. . . . I've learned that whenever I decide something with an open heart, I usually make the right decision. I've learned that even when I have pains, I don't want to be one. . . . I've learned that people will forget what you said, people will forget what you did, but people will never forget how you made them feel.*

While I've long loved the story of Jesus storming through the Jerusalem temple in a holy rage, there is another story that should be held in balance with it. It is the story of what Jesus does when Peter takes out a sword

*Quotation attributed to Maya Angelou from http://www.montana.edu/wrt /Don'tBreaktheElastic.doc, accessed October 11, 2016.

and, in anger over his beloved friend's betrayal and arrest, cuts off an ear of one of the soldiers who comes to arrest Jesus in the Garden of Gethsemane. Jesus here does not respond by praising the rage of his disciple. Rather, he responds by healing and restoring the ear of the soldier and by warning his disciple that "all who take the sword will perish by the sword" (Matt. 26:52).

His words are good reminders for us as well. Yes, there are times when our holy rage needs to be kindled over the larger causes of peace, justice, and righteousness in this world. But not all rage is holy. And sometimes the swords we draw in self-righteous defense may do us more harm than good, gutting us of the energy and strength we need for our own healing.

Scripture Readings: John 2:13–16; Matthew 26:47–52

For Further Reflection
— How would you distinguish between "holy rage" and anger that is not holy?
— Describe an experience when anger fueled you to take action that was good and of God.
— Describe a time when anger was debilitating for you, robbing you of energy and life and wholeness.
— Offer your rage and anger to God, asking God to show you when it is helpful and when you need to let it go.

WIGS, WIGS, WIGS

When my doctor first told me that I would need to have chemotherapy following surgery, I immediately began trying to picture myself with no hair. The thought—while not as horrifying as I might have imagined—was sobering nonetheless. I am too old to look good bald and too vain to think that turbans and hats alone will do the trick for me.

A couple of weeks after my surgery, as I eagerly anticipated a weekend visit from my daughter, a college senior, it suddenly dawned on me that a trip to a wig shop with this funky woman child might be an altogether different experience than a trip alone. In fact, trying on wigs with Leonora—whose own hair color in recent years has ranged from bright red to platinum to pink and who literally shaved her head just for the heck of it one summer (she reported having a beautiful head!)—might actually be fun. So I called the first shop listed on the flyer I had received from my local chapter of the Breast Cancer Society—a place called "Wigs, Wigs, Wigs"—and made an appointment to see Phyllis for a wig fitting in their private room the following Saturday afternoon.

The shop, located about fifteen miles from our home, did not impress me on first sight. The modest white building with peeling paint was located on an untraveled side street in a small town and had a general look of neglect about it. I muttered something to Leonora as we got out of the car about "doubting I would find anything here that I liked," but since she was with me and this was our one shot at mother-daughter wig shopping, I ventured inside.

Phyllis, a sixty-something-year-old woman with a warm smile, welcomed us to her shop and invited us to have a seat while she allowed time for another client—an elderly woman who had suffered a stroke and who moved very slowly with her walker—to exit the back room and make her way with her husband to her car. Then Phyllis ushered Leonora and me into that room and began pulling out wigs for my perusal.

Though the first few were too small for my head, I think it was only the third or fourth wig I tried on that caused me to breathe a huge sigh of relief. Not only did it fit; it actually looked like my hair and even blended well with wisps of my hair that were escaping underneath. Since I knew I had found one wig I could wear without undue embarrassment, the rest of the visit was sheer fun. Indeed Phyllis, getting into the spirit of this mother-daughter outing, began pulling out all sorts of wigs for me to try on: a shoulder-length, wavy, red wig; a poofy, dark brown wig; and a platinum-blonde, spiky, punk-rocker wig! (We all agreed this was *not* my look.)

In the end, Leonora pressed me to buy not one but two wigs: one for everyday and one for dress-up. "Pamper yourself, Momma," she said. "You deserve it." And we both left that shop, having been surprised—and not a little overwhelmed—by the grace we had experienced there.

It turns out that Phyllis has two sisters who have battled breast cancer. This shop is her ministry. Every Saturday afternoon for the past thirty years, she has opened her doors to "my chemo ladies" (as she refers to us). And with tender, loving care and lots of good humor, she helps those who are fighting disease and low self-esteem feel better about themselves by looking better. Indeed, we discovered that Phyllis had helped found the American Cancer Society's "Look Good, Feel Better" chapter in her county.

One of the things I am learning about life with cancer is that grace crops up in totally unexpected places—like a ramshackle-looking wig shop—and that kindness and good humor go a long way toward making an ordinary day one that is grace-filled. I am grateful for Phyllis, who ministers to chemo ladies each Saturday afternoon, and for Leonora, who ministered to me by her presence, her fun-loving spirit, and her encouragement that I pamper myself and buy two wigs. God is in the midst of this. Of that I am certain. And sometimes She blows me away by the sheer audacity of Her unexpected presence.

Scripture Reading: Galatians 5:22–23

For Further Reflection
— In Galatians, the fruit of the Spirit is identified as: "love, joy, peace, patience, kindness, generosity, faithfulness, gentleness, and self-control." Think of someone you know who quietly yet persistently embodies one or more of these traits in everyday life. What do you learn from her or his witness about the workings of the Spirit?

FACING CHEMOTHERAPY

I am not looking forward to chemotherapy. Although I know it is necessary for killing the cancer cells in my body, I also know that it kills lots of other good cells as well, including cells I need to fight off infection and disease.

My daughter and I had quite a discussion about chemotherapy a week or so ago. She kept saying she hated for me to have it, and I finally said to her, "Look, it's sort of like just-war theory [a theory that is sometimes used to help determine whether or not there is just cause to get involved in a war and, if so, how to fight it fairly]. You can either sit around and let those little, nasty cells destroy your body and do nothing. Or you can get down and dirty yourself—fighting it with chemicals that are harmful to all manner of living things but that also have a good chance of killing those harmful cells." We laughed about the analogy, but there's also a lot of truth in it.

Now that I'm feeling better and healing from surgery, now that I'm finally regaining energy and getting out and about some more, I dread the thought of taking toxic substances into my body that will make me sick. I dread the approaching long months of low energy, depleted physical strength, and a deficient immune system. I dread having a chemical taste in my mouth, feeling nauseated, and watching my hair—which beauticians have always admired for its texture, thickness, and body—fall out in clumps. I, who have never been a big medicine taker anyhow, dread sitting in some clinic, watching all sorts of foreign chemicals flow through an IV into my body and into my bloodstream. In short, I dread chemotherapy—no matter how much better they tell me it's gotten in recent years.

But I am quite clear that I am going to have it. Because the only cells that will be harmed by this war are my own, I am going to engage in the battle—hoping that by "fighting the good fight" I will live to share many more years with my husband, my children, and all those I hold dear. The short-term cost is definitely worth the long-term gain.

Yesterday, a pastor friend, who has herself faced breast cancer, sent me a note that included a wonderful Scripture passage for the battle ahead:

> I have called you by name, you are mine.
> When you pass through the waters, I will be with you;
>   and through the rivers, they shall not overwhelm you;
> when you walk through fire you shall not be burned,
>   and the flame shall not consume you.
> . . . .
> Because you are precious in my sight,
>   and honored, and I love you.
>
> (Isa. 43:1b–3, 4a)

What lovely images to take with me into the treatment room in the months ahead! I will cling fast to those promises, in hopes that these deep waters will not drown me and that this chemical fire—difficult though it will be to endure—will ultimately prove to be cleansing, purifying, and healing.

Scripture Reading: Isaiah 43:1–4

For Further Reflection
— Have you faced something that you knew was bad and potentially harmful for you on one level but ultimately could be good for you? What did you do?
— How do you interpret the images of "rivers" and "fire" in the Isaiah text?
— What do they represent in your own current life?

THE GLASS IS ⅛ FULL

My husband, Al, is an irrepressible optimist. And frankly, that's one of the things I love most about him. Sure, there are times when he drives me crazy with his unquenchable spirit, but on the whole, when Al enters a room, hope enters with him. That's a large part of what makes him such a wonderful husband, father, and pastor.

On the day of my first chemotherapy treatment, I was understandably apprehensive. The thought of all those toxic chemicals going into my body, the anxiety about potential side effects, and the knowledge that I had "bad veins" all added to my sense of fear as we approached the cancer treatment center. While my surgeon was going to insert a porta-catheter in my vein the following week, so that all subsequent injections could be made directly through it, today's treatment would be by a needle inserted into my arm. And I knew from my prior reading that the drug I would receive—often called the "red devil"—could cause serious burning and even permanent tissue damage if it leaked out of a vein and into my body.

Al and I intentionally arrived at the cancer treatment center at the hospital early and had a bowl of soup together before heading over for my chemo session. As we sat at the table, breaking bread together before beginning this next stage of treatment, Al looked across the table at me and said, "Just think, Nora. After today, you only have seven treatments to go." At first I just stared at him, incredulous that once again, my beloved spouse could be so positive in a difficult situation like this one. But as his words sank in and as I realized I was actually finding comfort in them (after all, seven treatments sounded a lot more manageable than six months' worth), I threw back my head and laughed. "Oh, Al," I said, "that has to be the most classic rendition of 'the glass is ½—or in this case—⅛ full' I have ever heard!" Whereupon Al chuckled and replied, "Yes, and you haven't even had the first one yet!"

Fred Craddock, one of my favorite preachers, once said that hope needs only one calorie a day to survive. It's so true. Take a meal shared over fear and anxiety and infuse it with a calorie of hope, and the whole tenor changes. Perhaps that's why Jesus spoke these words to his disciples while they sat at table, grieving his impending death and their great loss, "Do not let your hearts be troubled, and do not let them be afraid" (John 14:27). He knew that what God alone could offer was the one calorie of resurrection hope they all so desperately needed.

With the eyes of this world, the glass often looks ⅞ empty—or perhaps as if there's not a drop of hope left. But with the eyes of faith, we glimpse another reality: one full of promise and life and peace.

Scripture Reading: John 14:1–3

For Further Reflection
— What is the difference between optimism and hope? How are they related in your experience? How are they different?
— What is the "one calorie of hope" you have experienced this past week?
— To what specific situation in your life might Jesus be speaking those words in the Scripture reading from John 14:1, "Do not let your hearts be troubled"?

PIERCE'S WITNESS

When I went for my first chemotherapy session, I chose a seat in a sunny spot beside a young man who looked to be the same age as my two young adult children. I was deeply saddened to see someone so young in that room, and I kept thinking about him all through my own treatment. Finally, when the nurse had removed the needle from my vein, I turned to him and made eye contact, hoping to initiate conversation, if he were willing. Pierce (that was his name), who had obviously overheard me talking with my nurse, seemed eager to talk and said to me, "So, you have children?" I gladly talked with him about our two college-aged children—where they were studying, what they were majoring in—and then asked if he was a student.

"I was supposed to be a freshman at Rutgers this year," he said, "but this happened to me instead." He went on to tell me that in October of last year—just after beginning freshman year—he was diagnosed with esophageal cancer, a rare form of cancer affecting about 1 percent of the U.S. population. He had no idea anything was wrong with him until, over a two-week time period, he became increasingly unable to eat or drink anything. The doctors then discovered a massive tumor, located at the juncture of his stomach and esophagus. Rather than operating immediately, his oncologist first prescribed a five-week course of radiation and chemotherapy, hoping both to shrink the cancer and to prevent it from metastasizing elsewhere in his body. Unfortunately, that first round of treatment failed to do him any good, and the cancer had already metastasized in his liver. So he was now undergoing a second round with different drugs.

This young man had everything to be bitter and angry

about. But bitter was not his *modus operandi.* In fact, he often gazed off into space as he spoke, talking honestly about the way in which this cancer had totally disrupted his life but also talking with warmth and good humor about what it had taught him. At one point he even softly said, "Actually, this cancer is a gift."

"What were you planning to major in at Rutgers?" I asked, hoping to learn more about this "gift."

"Well," he replied with a grin. "It's sorta funny. Before all this happened, I had my life all mapped out. I was planning to be a business and finance major, and my ultimate goal was to become CEO of a Fortune 500 company. I love math and thought that was the way I would go."

"And now?" I asked.

"Now," he said, "I'm sort of drawn to this," as he waved his hand around toward the room of competent and compassionate nurses who were ministering to us chemo patients. "I'm thinking I'd really like to go into pre-med and become a doctor."

I was reminded, as he spoke, of one of the books that someone had given me, *Now That I Have Cancer, I Am Whole.* Throughout the volume, author John Robert McFarland, who himself underwent a lengthy battle with colon cancer, tells of all the ways in which cancer forced him to reprioritize his life, sorting out the peripherals from the essentials and making conscious decisions about how to live out the rest of his days in meaningful and fulfilling ways. He, too, frequently speaks of cancer as a "gift"—and though I do not for a second believe that our loving God sends cancer to a nineteen-year-old college student (or to a fifty-one-year-old woman, for that matter) to teach us lessons we might have learned otherwise, I do have great belief in a God who can take whatever difficulties life deals us and use them for God's good and gracious purposes.

In the biblical story of Joseph, there is a wonderful scene in which Joseph, now a prince in Pharaoh's court in

Egypt, is reunited with his brothers who years before had sold him into slavery in a fit of jealous rage. In one of those power reversals that can happen in life (and are common to the Bible), Joseph, formerly the weak brother, has now become the most powerful and literally holds his family's life in his hands (given the famine in Canaan and Joseph's access to the Egyptian grain supply). The brothers, who have come to plead for food with this ruler in Pharaoh's court, at first do not recognize Joseph. They assumed he died years before. When they finally do recognize him, they cower in his presence, fearful of the revenge he might exact.

But Joseph has moved to an altogether different place in his spirit. He says to them, "Come closer to me. . . . I am your brother, Joseph, whom you sold into Egypt. And now do not be distressed, or angry with yourselves, because you sold me here; for God sent me before you to preserve life" (Gen. 45:4–5).

In another passage, Joseph makes an amazing theological affirmation, which also cuts to the heart of the Gospel's good news: "Even though you intended to do harm to me," he says to his brothers, "God intended it for good" (50:20).

I think that what Pierce and John Robert McFarland, and others who have walked this path before me, sense is that while cancer itself is certainly "evil" and not of God, God often means it—and uses it—for good. It can be a gift, if we are willing to receive and welcome it as such.

Scripture Reading: Genesis 45:1–15

For Further Reflection
— Name before God some of the "gifts" that are coming to you through your struggle with illness or other difficulties.
— As you look back on your life, describe instances in which you believe God has taken evil and used it (ultimately) for your good.

WHEN THROUGH
THE DEEP WATERS

The week after my first chemo treatment proved to be the week when, more than any other since all this began, Al and I began to feel that the waters of chaos (literally!) were about to overwhelm us. On the Saturday following my first treatment, it poured rain all day in our town on top of the twenty-four inches of snow we had received the previous weekend. Al and I kept checking the basement regularly, since we were worried some of the water might leak in.

At 5:00 p.m. when we left to go to the home of friends for dinner, our basement was dry. When we returned from dinner at 9:00 p.m. (I was feeling shaky and nauseated and very tired from the treatment), we had two feet of muddy, cold water flowing through our basement—where our furnace, hot water heater, and brand-new chest freezer were all located, along with family keepsakes and furniture we were storing for our children.

We finally found an emergency plumber who came late that night and installed another sump pump; ours had burned out trying to handle the flood. We also spent three hours trying to salvage family photos that had been stored in boxes on shelves in the basement and were now soaking wet. By the wee, small hours of Sunday morning (the timing could not have been worse for my pastor husband), there was hardly an inch of floor space in our house that was not covered with drying photos.

As we later discovered, a water main up the hill from us had broken during the storm, sending torrential waters through our next-door neighbor's yard and then through ours. Indeed, our yard now looks like a stream bed, and you can easily see where the river parted and flowed around either side of our house, carving out gullies and dumping dirt and gravel as it went. Fortunately the water company has taken responsibility for this disaster and sent a clean-up crew to our house this past week to begin hosing down and cleaning up the mess. But the basement is still full of waterlogged stuff.

It is simply too much—in the midst of everything else we are dealing with right now—and there have been times when I was so overwhelmed by it all I could only sit and weep. As I told several friends this week, I have no interest whatsoever in auditioning for the part of Job. Enough already!

But there is also a very fitting hymn stanza that keeps running through my head, giving me comfort:

When through the deep waters I call thee to go,
The rivers of sorrow shall not overflow;
For I will be near thee, thy troubles to bless,
And sanctify to thee thy deepest distress.*

Meanwhile there are some things for which I am particularly grateful right now: my hair has not yet fallen out, my doctors and nurses are an incredibly competent group, my church job recently gave me the opportunity to hear Archbishop Desmond Tutu speak about his vision of a world at peace, and the ongoing love of family and friends sustains me daily on this journey.

Today is Ash Wednesday, and I am probably more aware this year than any other of my mortality: Ashes to ashes, dust to dust. That's how it will someday be for all of us. Meanwhile, I'm grateful for each day of life that I

---

*"How Firm a Foundation," *The Presbyterian Hymnal* (Louisville, KY: Westminster/ John Knox, 1990), 361.

am given, and for the promise of life everlasting. God is good—and all *shall* be well.

Scripture Reading: Psalm 69:1–15

For Further Reflection
— When the waters of life threaten to overwhelm you, where do you turn for comfort and encouragement?
— Is there a favorite poem or hymn or Scripture passage that sees you through?
— Where do you envision God being at such a time?

LOOKING AND FEELING
LIKE A CHEMO LADY

For the past few weeks, friends and colleagues have been telling me that my problem is that I don't look sick. Despite the very real battle that has been going on in my body, I have looked the picture of perfect health: rosy cheeks, full head of hair, and my usual smile spread across my face. Because people at work see me only on my better days of the week (trying for all the world to look and act like my old self), they haven't seen me at my lowest ebb.

But the past few days have changed all of that. I am finally beginning to look like a full-fledged chemo lady, and it is depressing, to say the least.

My hair started falling out on Sunday. I could almost tell it was going to happen because my head actually ached that morning when I awoke—not on the inside, but across the surface. As if it was dead and just waiting to be buried. And when I ran my fingers through it, I always came out with a full clump of hair.

For some reason, I haven't been able yet to part with my hair. I've been storing it in little piles around the house and then gathering them together in a plastic bag. A friend told me the birds would probably love to have my hair for building their nests, and perhaps I will share it with them. But for now I'm not ready to part with this dying part of myself. I simply want to keep it around and cherish it— like you cherish a beloved body before burying it.

By yesterday, my head finally looked awful. The bald spots were readily apparent all over my scalp, and there was no longer any illusion that I had a full head of hair— even of the thinning variety. I am even thinking of doing that which I've been dreading: going to my beautician and getting her to shave it all off. If I want to begin wearing wigs, I'm going to have to get this old hair out of the way. But oh, I hate to see it go.

To add insult to injury, my body feels like my hair looks. I had my second round of chemo treatments this week, followed by my worst night yet: unrelenting nausea and vomiting until the wee small hours, times when I felt like my stomach was literally turning inside out. I looked like death warmed over—pallid, sickly, and wretched.

Enter Mimi. Mimi is a friend from our church who volunteers at the cancer center where I receive treatments. She was going over to the center yesterday and offered to take me for an injection I was scheduled to have. But when I arrived I discovered that my nurse was going to give me more than the injection to build up my blood count; she was also going to give me an IV to up my body fluids and try to replenish some of the energy I had lost through the previous night's nausea and vomiting.

I felt bad for Mimi. She hadn't bargained for a two-hour trip to the doctor. But somehow she managed to turn those lemons into lemonade. She got permission from a nurse to put me on a portable IV pack, and then she walked me downstairs with her for a private showing of hats and turbans in the cancer center's "Image Enhancement Center." While the IV steadily dripped into my vein, Mimi and I tried on all sorts of hats, "halos" (rings of hair that look for all the world like a monk's tonsure), and bangs to see how we might improve my failing appearance. And oh, what a joy it was to see my chemo head transformed into a more presentable (and more youthful!) appearance. I ended up buying four hats and one halo (at bargain prices, I might add); just knowing they are there strengthens my resolve to get my head shaved. I now have something present-able—even attractive—to wear when the last vestiges of my beloved mop go. Something to wear to work, something to wear on my head in the cold weather, something to wear around the house and to sleep, and even something to wear while working in the yard in summertime.

I thank God for Mimi today—and for all the volunteers and caring people who try to make life better for those of us going through this ordeal. The Scriptures tell us that God created us—every one of us—in God's own image and called us "very good." But sometimes it's hard to believe we're "very good" when we look in the mirror and see not the self we've been used to seeing but a vastly altered and sickened image of ourselves. Thankfully, the Mimi's of the world have the grace to help us love the self that still resides within—the self that God is always the first to see and love.

Scripture Reading: Genesis 1:27, 31

For Further Reflection
— Think of a time in your life (perhaps even now) when it's been very difficult to love yourself. What is/was it about yourself that you found difficult to accept and embrace?
— What does it mean to you and your self-image to have a God who created you, called you by name, and pronounced you "very good" (Gen. 1:31)?

LIONS AND TIGERS
AND BEARS

Some days, in my fight for wholeness, I confess that the lions and tigers and bears threaten to overwhelm me—as they did the Tin Man on his way to Oz. Yesterday was one of those days.

I awoke feeling lousy—nauseated and tired and generally sick all over—since the chemotherapy drugs, received two days prior, were assaulting my body. I did not want to go to the hospital for the MUGA scan that my doctor had prescribed, a close radiological reading of the heart that would tell my physician whether or not this first round of chemotherapy treatments had done damage to my heart muscles. Nor did I want to go to her office for four more hours of IV fluids, even though I knew they would eventually make me feel better. And frankly I did not want to spend another day around sick people. What I wanted to do was stay home in bed, nestled under the covers, reading my novel about the bubonic plague—which, ironically, I kept hoping would eventually offer some word of grace to a plagued world.

But when duty calls in this relentless health regimen, you go. And so I did. I got myself over to the hospital waiting room and managed to read a few more depressing chapters in my book while waiting for my MUGA scan. I made it through the scan just fine. But by the end of the morning, my stomach was roiling. So I stopped by the hospital cafe and bought a take-out container of chicken noodle soup, hoping to appease my queasiness by sipping it during my long afternoon.

I was well prepared, I thought, for this session—as prepared as I could possibly be. It wasn't until I sat down in a comfortable chair in the large, sunny room where my chemotherapy and IV sessions take place, that I lost it. The tears started rolling down my cheeks of their own accord, and my body heaved with sobs. Try as I might, I could not stop the flow of grief and despair.

My nurse—incredibly compassionate and kind—was a bit taken aback, since ordinarily my disposition in the treatment room is sunny. She gently asked if I wanted her to get the doctor and also asked if I was often depressed during these treatments. I told her no on both counts, but I also told her that the day was proving to be overwhelming for me. There was too much to be done and too much possible terror to be encountered, especially on a day when I felt absolutely and completely lousy to begin with.

She brought me a box of tissues, began the IV that would send the anti-nausea medicine into my veins, laid an afghan over my lap to warm me when the IV fluids made me cold, pulled the lever at the side of my chair so that my feet could be comfortably propped up, and told me to lay back and relax—that the medicines would soon make me sleep.

As I lay there, I thought of the email I had received just the day before from my wonderfully encouraging daughter. "You're tough, you know, Momma," she had written to me, "tough even if you don't feel like it."

Yesterday I felt less than tough. I felt like a coward who needed a new heart, like a tin man who lacked a soul, and like Dorothy who had been slung far away from home and set on a tortuous journey with no end in sight. I felt broken, beaten down, and afraid. And I felt sad—enormously sad for all that I had lost and might be losing to this disease.

Eventually I slept. The medicines and the crying and the sheer exhaustion of the day wore me out, and I slept. And when I awoke, I felt more peaceful.

"You're tough, Momma." I could hear my daughter

proudly saying to me as I walked out the door into the late afternoon—another grueling day of treatments behind me. "Tough even if you don't feel like it."

"Tough" is not usually how I feel these days. Yet at some tender place, some place deep down within my fearful heart, I wondered yesterday if I might actually begin believing in my daughter's vision of me. Perhaps I could be tough. Perhaps God is making me tough. And perhaps lions and tigers and bears are not so threatening after all. For once again, I have been surrounded and upheld by a prior and far more powerful grace.

Scripture Reading: Romans 5:1–5

For Further Reflection

— Reflect on those places in your own life where you are despairing and in need of a new heart.
— What are the voices and who are the people around you that give you hope and renewed courage for the journey?
— In Romans 5:5, Paul asserts that "hope does not disappoint us." Do you believe that is true? Why or why not?
— In what or in whom do you place hope?

THANK GOD FOR LUMPS

I was sure I had misheard him. But when I asked him to repeat what he had said, he said it again, "I thank God for lumps."

I might have written off this comment had it come from another, as some highly insensitive male response to a woman with breast cancer; but in this case, to do so was impossible. For this man actually lost his beloved wife to breast cancer over five years ago. Though we hadn't seen each other for many more years than that, he had called to tell me he was praying for me after hearing about my cancer.

Harry (my friend) and Cathy were members of one of four congregations in a yoked parish where my husband and I first served as copastors after graduating from seminary. Cathy and I went through the excitement of our first pregnancies together, laughing over the indignity of having to waddle through the woods behind that country church on Sunday morning to use the outhouse (there was no indoor plumbing in the old wood-frame meeting house, built in 1747) and rejoicing with each other when our first children—both daughters—were born only a few months apart. One of my favorite pregnancy photos is of Cathy and me, standing back-to-back in my yard after a joint baby shower, posing in profile, with our big bellies proudly stuck out in front of us. Our Leonora and their Rebecca shared many happy hours in their infancy and toddler-hood, playing on a blanket in the back of the sanctuary. (There was no nursery in those days either.)

While Al and I intentionally stopped at two children, Cathy and Harry—who lived on a farm and always wanted a brood—eventually had four: two girls and two boys. After our little congregation took a large leap of faith and built its first-ever addition to the sanctuary—a free-standing, multipurpose building with a fellowship hall, classroom space, a nursery, and indoor plumbing—Cathy took even more children under her wing. She founded and taught in that congregation's first childcare center.

When we received word of Cathy's cancer and, somewhat later, of her death, it broke our hearts. This woman of faith was much beloved by many—including us. To think of Harry and those four wonderful children living life without her was almost more than we could bear.

So Harry's call meant a lot to me. We took our time on the phone that Saturday morning, catching up on each other's lives and children, rekindling the flames of an old and treasured friendship. Harry even told me, toward the end of our conversation, that there is another woman in his life—someone who lost her own husband to cancer—and that while he's taking it slow, he's also grateful for this possibility of new life and love on the horizon.

It was near the very end of our conversation—when I told him how shocked I had been that my own small, malignant lump had been discovered during a routine mammogram—that Harry quietly replied, "I thank God for lumps."

"Why?" I asked somewhat incredulously, after first making sure I had heard him correctly.

"Because," he replied. "Cathy didn't have any. She had one of those rare kinds of inflammatory cancer that travels throughout your system but that doesn't cause lumps. So by the time we discovered her cancer, the doctors figured it had been working its damage for well over four years."

Today I'm thanking God for lumps, too, and for mammograms. They may not bring the news we want, but oh, how much better—in the long run—to know, to catch it early, and to have some chance of living a longer life with those we love the most.

Prayer

Thank you, O God, for lumps. Thank you for advances in medical science that allow for early detection of this dread disease, for new treatments that are constantly being tested and discovered, and for medical professionals who give us news that helps us face reality, even when we don't want to hear it.

Bless all those, we pray, who are suffering from detection that did not come early enough and who are now facing great suffering and even death. Hear us now as we name those known to us before you . . . Hold us all in the hollow of your hand, and grant us your healing, your wholeness, your peace.

Especially comfort and give grace to those who mourn the loss of those they have loved to this disease. May they know the hope of new life that comes only from you.

Through Jesus Christ our Lord, Amen.

THE PUPPY WITHIN

I have such ambivalence toward this cancer. There are days when I simply cannot wait until the treatments are finished so that I can get on with my "normal" life—life as it used to be. And there are days when I actually dread the end of the treatments, because somehow, in the midst of them, I have known a depth of faith and trust, a sense of peace and the presence of God, that I have not known before. I do not want to lose it.

Today those feelings are all mixed up together. Today I begin a new round of chemotherapy, and—as is the case with most chemotherapy—I dread it. I hate what these drugs do to my body, and the particular drug I will receive today has all sorts of potential allergic reactions and side effects that sound decidedly unpleasant. The thought of my muscles aching, of the nerves in my fingers and toes tingling or losing feeling altogether, the possibility that my blood pressure might plummet or that my body might swell or break into hives—these are not my ideas of a good time. If this cup could pass from me, I would surely will it.

But I also know—based on my experiences these past weeks and months—that somehow, some way, God will see me through. In this next stage of cancer treatment, as in the last, I will come to know God more fully, more deeply, more truly than before. And toward that reality, I genuinely yearn.

In my devotional reading this morning, I ran across a writing of C. S. Lewis that captures something of what I am feeling and experiencing. Lewis writes about the fact that often we are progressing along in life, going on our merry way, until something happens to set us back so that "all my little happinesses look like broken toys." At such times, says Lewis, "I remind myself that all these toys were never intended to possess my heart, that my true good is in another world and my only real treasure is Christ." He continues:

> And perhaps by God's grace, I succeed, and for a day or two become a creature consciously dependent on God and drawing its strength from the right sources. But the moment the threat is withdrawn, my whole nature leaps back to the toys: I am even anxious, God forgive me, to banish from my mind the only thing that supported me under the threat because it is now associated with the misery of those few days. . . . Like a puppy when the hated bath is over—I shake myself dry as I can and run off to reacquire my comfortable dirtiness, if not in the nearest manure heap, at least in the nearest flower bed.*

How like that puppy I am! I'm ready to bolt as soon as possible and frolic in the flower bed with my toys, which probably would not be such a bad things were I not also in danger of losing, in the process, that sense of absolute dependence on my Creator God.

So here's the challenge. How do we live life faithfully with lots of toys? How do we go back to cancer-free (or crisis-free) existence and still cling to God as if God is all we have?

The problem, I suppose, is as old as idolatry itself, as old as the golden calf, as old as the first commandment. How do we keep the good, created order and all the gifts it offers—work, recreation, relationships, vacations, nature, beauty, time—from usurping the place that is due

*C. S. Lewis from *The Problem of Pain*, as quoted in Benedict J. Groeschel, CFR, with Kevin Perrota, eds., *The Journey toward God: In the Footsteps of the Great Spiritual Writers—Catholic, Protestant, and Orthodox* (Ann Arbor, MI: Charis, Servant Publications, 2000), 78–79.

God alone. Hopefully if we practice living life rooted and grounded in God long enough, we will learn some things about living life in God when the toys are returned to us. At least if we find ourselves wallowing in blissful glee in the flower bed, it will be with an eye turned in gratitude toward heaven.

Scripture Readings: Exodus 20:1–6; Psalm 62:5–8

For Further Reflection

— Can you remember a time in your life when your reliance on God and God alone was absolute? What difference did that reality make in your relationship with God, with others, and in your spiritual life in general?
— Are there things in your life currently that keep you from serving God and God alone? How are you tempted to "idolatry," and what steps might you need to take in order to reorient yourself toward loving God above all else?

Prayer

For you alone, O God, my soul waits in silence, for you are my rock, my salvation, and my fortress. Upon you rests my deliverance, and in you I put my sure trust. Teach me, O God, to place my life in your safe keeping, not only when times are bad, but also when times are good. Teach me to trust you at all times, and not only when times are tough. Teach me to pour my heart out to you in prayer, not only in those seasons when lament comes easily to my tongue, but also in those seasons when flowers and freedom overwhelm me with wonder and joy. For you are the God of my deliverance, my only hope, and my salvation. Amen.

THE WOUNDED HEALER

I am often reminded these days of Henri Nouwen's book *The Wounded Healer*, because I am now learning firsthand that brokenness does indeed attract brokenness in Christian vocation. I began a new venture in ministry this year in January, the same month in which I was diagnosed with breast cancer. At first I could only shake my fist at the timing, because I had been extremely excited about this new call of God upon my life and was eager to jump in with my whole being to undertake the tasks before me. The last thing I wanted was a serious illness to impinge on my ability to function well.

But cancer, as I quickly learned, is no respecter of clocks or calls or plans. It has its own timing, and ordinary activities of life and ministry simply have to learn to get in line behind the more pressing matters like doctors' appointments, medical tests, surgeries, and treatments — not to mention the enormous energy required for healing itself.

My first response to cancer was a woeful, "This cancer is seriously messing up my life! I don't like it at all!"

Yet I have come to see in subsequent weeks that cancer is also opening me to possibilities for a much deeper sharing of life and faith with others than I would have dreamed possible. As word of my disease has filtered out to a broader public and a broader church, friends and acquaintances in unexpected places have also shared with me — in remarkable candor — the brokenness of their lives.

A dear friend from college days and I have regularly emailed about her divorce, and the pain, guilt, and sense of failure she feels in its wake. An acquaintance I barely know, from a professional society of which we are both a part, wrote about the lawsuit his church is facing, and the angst and pain he and his broken community are suffering. Two other professional colleagues have written about tests their young adult sons are undergoing for life-threatening diseases. And I regularly have conversation with my new parishioners—a choir member undergoing treatment for HIV/AIDS, two men recently diagnosed with prostate cancer, a woman recovering from a brain tumor, and a woman who has been struggling with severe depression and mental illness for years—about their ongoing challenges.

I have been moved by the depth of self-revelation in these conversations, levels that I do not think would have been achieved so quickly had not these dear folk sensed in me an increased level of empathy and openness due to my own illness. And while, in prior years, I might have felt overwhelmed by their heartaches—wondering how I would bear their manifold burdens on top of my own—I feel differently now. For one thing, I don't feel that I have to be their problem solver; indeed, I know that I can't be. So instead, I just try to be a friend, a listener, and a partner in prayer. For another, I have become, through the years, well aware of my limitations as a counselor, so I don't try to be who and what I'm not. I am much quicker than I used to be to refer people with significant needs to the specially trained pastors, counselors, or social workers who can meet their needs far better than I. And finally, I have come to see, through my own illness, that the very best gifts I can offer to others are my prayers for their healing. In addition to the prayers I offer for them when we are together, I add the name of each one to my daily prayer list, praying for them by name and entrusting them into the hands of God. This discipline also helps me keep their names and concerns on my heart so that I do not forget to speak a word of concern or empathy when next I see them.

Frankly, all of this has given me a very ambivalent feeling about my cancer. Some days I am so grateful for these new openings for ministry, which cancer has afforded me, that I wonder how I will function when it is gone. Cancer, in this regard, has been a gift in my life. Yet I also hope and trust that even when it is in remission (as I surely hope it will be), I will still bear in my body its scars, its memories, and those marks that will hereafter brand me as a "wounded healer."

The apostle Paul bore in his body a "thorn in the flesh" that caused him pain and discomfort throughout his ministry but that also afforded him a renewed sense of compassion for all the suffering ones to whom he ministered (see 2 Cor. 12:7). I earnestly pray that my "thorn"—those toxic cancer cells that are wreaking havoc in my body—will be exorcised from my flesh through the long months of chemotherapy and radiation treatments I am having to endure. But I also pray that the wounds that remain after this disease is in remission will link me more closely with Christ's own wounds and with the wounds of this broken world for which he died.

Scripture Reading: 2 Corinthians 12:7b–10

For Further Reflection
— Reflect on a time in your life or the life of someone you know when what you deemed to be a weakness was used by God for something strong and good. What did you learn from this experience about God's capacity to show forth strength in the midst of human weakness?

Prayer
Help me to see in each new day, O God, those other wounded ones who cross my path, and especially those to

whom you would have me make myself present. Use my "thorn in the flesh" as an opening to a deeper sharing of life and faith with others and to a deeper sensitivity to their pain and the pain of this world. Save me from thinking I need to save others, and remind me that that work is yours alone. Make me bold and persistent in prayer, trusting all those for whom I care to the safe-keeping of your loving and healing arms. Through Christ our Lord, Amen.

THE HEALING POWER
OF WATER

∽∾

(Age 61: written ten years after my battle with cancer)

Yesterday, two dear friends came for an overnight visit. They were married seven years ago. She, a successful attorney, finally found this love of her life after two failed marriages and dearly treasures her relationship with this man who is now her husband. He is now battling incurable kidney cancer.

After an afternoon sail with brisk breezes (which our male friend especially enjoyed since he grew up racing sailboats), my husband and I prepared dinner while our friends sat on a deck looking out onto the harbor. I could tell that just sitting there, soaking up the sights and the sounds of the water was calming for both of them.

There is something about water that brings healing to the soul and body. It is no wonder that the ancients sought out springs that were said to have healing powers and traveled long distances to bathe in them; or that a man in one of Jesus' healing stories sat by the pool of Bethzatha for many years, hoping that someone would lift him into the water so that he could be healed (John 5:2–9).

The biblical story in 2 Kings 5, of Naaman, commander of the Syrian army, has long intrigued me. Though Naaman believed in the healing power of water, he didn't believe God could use just *any* water to bring healing. When Elisha, the prophet of Israel, told Naaman to go and wash seven times in the Jordan River of Israel if he wanted to be healed, Naaman balked. "What's wrong with the Syrian rivers?" he asked. "Couldn't I wash in them and be cleansed?"

My guess is that Naaman, a man used to commanding armies, didn't want to humble himself and wash in a small, insignificant (to him at least) foreign river. If healing was to come, he wanted it to be big and bold and splashy and on his own home turf. Indeed, he was so enraged by the prophet's injunction, he almost missed healing altogether.

Until, that is, his servants intervened and convinced him to give it a try. And sure enough, after seven times dipping in the Jordan, we read that "his flesh was restored like the flesh of a young boy, and he was clean" (v. 14b).

The television evangelists of my childhood (such as A. A. Allen and Oral Roberts) used to make it look like healing was big and splashy and sudden. They would lay hands on the part of the body that was ailing and command the disease to be healed in the name of God. And then people would miraculously be able to walk or hear or see.

But in my experience, the healing process usually has a lot more in common with dipping in the muddy Jordan waters than with television miracles. Take my friend, for instance. Every ninety days he has to go for another CT scan to see whether and where the cancer has reappeared in his body. Every day he has to take a medication that makes his hair turn white and his skin hypersensitive to the sun. He is fatigued a lot of the time and says he is losing his upper body strength. His doctor told him to expect to feel like he's aged ten years—and indeed he does.

But still, in faith and humility, he does what he is told he must do to help the healing process. He regularly dips in the Jordan, and whether a cure comes or not, I sense that already a new healing, a new wholeness, has taken over his being. He is calm, he is at peace, and he soaks up the wonders of this earth—including the beauty of a harbor at sunset—as if sealing it on his memory for all eternity.

Scripture Reading: 2 Kings 5:1–14

For Further Reflection

— Think about a time in your life or the life of a loved one when water has proved to be a healing force. What made it so?

— Pray for those you know who are in need of healing — that they may find the peace and the calm that can come from God — even while dipping seven times in the Jordan.

CONFRONTING THE BEAST

꩜꩜

(Age 61: written ten years after my battle with cancer)

Three of my friends are struggling with cancer right now. One of them—a dear friend from college days—has recently been told that her uterine cancer of two years ago has returned. Her fourteen-year-old adopted child and her life partner love her dearly, as do we, a close group of friends who recently gathered to lay hands on her and pray for her. As we concluded our time of prayer by singing together her two favorite hymns—"Great Is Thy Faithfulness" and "Be Thou My Vision"—we were reminded anew of the goodness and healing power of our God and of the faith that sustains us morning by morning, day by day.

My second friend just graduated from seminary—a task that she juggled while caring for four children and her semi-invalid father-in-law, who recently moved in with their family. Life was at last stretched out before her with new possibilities—she was awarded two prizes at graduation for her excellence as a preacher and was just this past week ordained a deacon in the Episcopal Church. But in the midst of it all came the unexpected diagnosis: Stage 2 breast cancer . . . Aggressive . . . Treatment required immediately. Next week she will have a double mastectomy, followed by "oodles of chemo." She wrote this morning that her challenge now is how to be "a good bald deacon."

The third friend is preparing to die. He has been told that his pancreatic cancer is incurable and that he has only a few months to live. In a couple of weeks, we will go to a choral evensong service he has planned at a chapel he loves to celebrate the end of his life. He alternates these days between walking bravely and boldly toward death and struggling to find homeopathic treatments that might prolong his days.

If you ask me to describe in this life "the beast" from the Scriptures, I would say its name is Cancer (with a capital C). It raises its ugly head at random, roaring out its threats, and striking whoever happens to be in its path. It is a hideously deceptive menace, employing stealth missile attacks on healthy bodies as it implants them with hidden bombs that threaten to detonate if not detected in time.

I hate cancer: Hate it, hate it, hate it. And frankly, I think God does, too. For Cancer takes something good that God created—cells that are meant to give life—distorts them, and then uses them to attack all that is good and healthy and whole within us.

The Scriptures tell us that only one power can defeat "the beast" and that is why prayer is so critically important in the fight against cancer. We are up against principalities and powers here, and while, of course, we call on all the wisdom and insight medical science can offer us in this battle (Thanks be to God for doctors and nurses and scientific researchers who devote their lives to battling this disease!), we also cry out to God in prayer, storming heaven's gates and calling on all the forces God has to muster in this cosmic battle against evil. While the ultimate victory is assured, the beast in this life continues to raise its hideous head.

Our calling is not to lose heart. Instead let us stand together, clasping the hands of our friends, staring the beast in the face, and singing through our tears with all the boldness we can muster:

Great is thy faithfulness, O God Creator,
There is no shadow of turning with thee;

Thou changest not, thy compassions they fail not,
As thou hast been, thou forever wilt be.*

Let us celebrate the bald deacons who will take us to the altars of this world, where we will taste the bread and drink the cup that assure us that the Lamb did indeed go up against the Beast; and though Christ suffered there with and for us, he also won the ultimate victory.

And let us revel in the beauty of a choral evensong, where the music and prayers take us to the very gates of heaven itself, where we even overhear the angels singing, "Blessing, and honour, and glory, and power, be unto him that sitteth upon the throne, and unto the Lamb for ever and ever" (Rev. 5:13 KJV).

Scripture Reading: Revelation 5:11–14

For Further Reflection
— Pray for all of those known to you who are battling the Cancer Beast, and write their names below.
— Pray also for all healthcare professionals and scientists who are working to cure cancer. Name those who are known to you.
— Give thanks to God for the lives of those whose battle against that beast here on earth has ended but who now live forever with God.

*Thomas Obediah Chisholm, "Great Is Thy Faithfulness," © 1923, Ren. 1951 Hope Publishing Company, Carol Stream, IL 60188. All rights reserved. Used by permission.

DISCIPLINES AND GIFTS OF THE SPIRIT

(WRITTEN AT AGES 58–63)

GRACE AND GRATITUDE

I have friends who go each year to the sea on Maryland's coast. They have named the place they stay there "Gratitude." Gratitude. What a perfect name for a spot on this earth where we are privileged to glimpse the wonders of God's creation and where that which wells up within us is sheer awe and wonder and thanksgiving for the gift of being alive and being right where we are.

I experience that emotion-too-deep-for-words when we are by the sea in Connecticut, where in the early morning I get to watch the geese come in early to feed in the cove, the swallows swooping low over the marsh as they search for bugs, local fisher people trolling for breakfast, and the rising sun turning the cobalt gray of the water to silver and mauve and deep hues of purple.

Gratitude: A sure sense that it is God who has made us and the whole world, and not we ourselves. Recognition that grace abounds in this universe of ours and that our very lives are dependent on it. An expression of wonder and awe and praise that bubbles from a well deep within us and overflows in sighs and prayers too deep for words.

When we live our lives in gratitude, we live out of a different center than does much of the world around us. I think of people I have known in my life—people who have very little in terms of this world's riches and who will never have the luxury of spending much time by the sea; people who have struggled with all kinds of challenges and hardships and setbacks—yet who choose, instead, to live lives in gratitude. And oh, what a difference it makes! Rather than focusing on what they don't have, they focus on what they do have and are quick to tell you about the many ways God has blessed them. Rather than becoming bitter when life does not go their way, they appreciate the small mercies that grace their daily lives. Rather than railing at the unfairness of the world, they extol the goodness and faithfulness of God. Their witness makes me want to be more grateful too—not only when it is easy, but also when struggling with a difficult challenge, when dealing with a major disappointment, or when confronted by an overwhelming loss.

The singer Olivia Newton John called one of her record albums *Grace and Gratitude*, and surely the two are connected. For when we live our lives in gratitude, it is as if we have put on 3-D glasses that enable us to view the world as infused with grace rather than as flat and closed and colorless. All of a sudden, through eyes of faith, we are able to see the mauves and the silvers and the deep purples that have been right there in front of us all the time.

I have long wondered what the difference was between the one leper who went back to thank Jesus for his healing, and the other nine who did not (see Luke 17). Surely all of them must have been overjoyed to have clean skin once again. Yet only one of them—the Samaritan—seemed to recognize the grace at the heart of it all. And it was to that one alone that Jesus also said, "Get up and go on your way; your faith has made you well" (v. 19). All had been cured, but only one, through gratitude, had been made whole.

While gratitude may come more naturally to some of us than to others, it is a spiritual practice we can also nurture in our lives. What a difference it would make to start each day by naming all those things we have to be thankful for in the past twenty-four hours, rather than by listing all the things we need to get done in the next twenty-four. What a difference it would make if we paused—in the midst of an overwhelming day—to put on those 3-D glasses and count our blessings. And what a difference it would make if we, like the tenth leper, made a practice of regularly saying "thank you" to God—not only for the big miracles we experience in our lives but also for the small graces.

Jesus wants to make all of us whole. So perhaps we need to rename the houses in our own hearts "gratitude."

Scripture Reading: Luke 17:11–19

For Further Reflection
— Make a list of the things that have occurred within the past twenty-four hours for which you are especially grateful, and give thanks to God for them. Consider keeping a prayer journal, and start each day by spending a few minutes naming and writing down your thanksgivings to God.

HUMOR

My dad turned ninety-two yesterday. And my mom threw him a party in the hall of the retirement home where they live. In the midst of a table set with cake and nuts and punch, she placed a sign that read: "Growing older means the blessing of looking back on where we've come from . . . looking forward to where we're going . . . and still having no idea where we parked the car."

So much of life—including aging—goes better with a dose of humor. I often tell students in my preaching classes that while *jokes* are usually inappropriate in the pulpit (since they are often unrelated to the sermon topic and also have some person or group of people as their "brunt"), *humor* is welcome. Indeed, I find that the preachers who can laugh with their congregations are often much beloved by them. They tend to take themselves less seriously and evidence a lighter side that draws people toward them.

The Bible doesn't say much overtly about humor. But for those who have eyes to see, the seeds of God's humor are definitely present. From the opening pages of Genesis—where God creates animals as diverse and funny-looking as walruses, platypuses, and baboons—to the closing pages of Revelation—where God defeats evil not with might and power but with a sacrificed and bleeding Lamb (the Greek actually implies a "lambkin")—God's sense of humor comes through.

Humor in the Scriptures also shows up in subtle ways—through irony, wordplays, or exaggerated imagery. I still remember the night when I was in high school, and our church youth group leader—in an attempt to compel

Brady, the most recalcitrant boy in our group, to participate—assigned him the evening devotional. Brady got his
revenge by going straight to Song of Solomon (also called
Song of Songs), where he read aloud:

> Your hair is like a flock of goats,
>   moving down the slopes of Gilead.
> Your teeth are like a flock of shorn ewes
>   that have come up from the washing,
> . . . .
> Your cheeks are like halves of a pomegranate.
> . . . .
> Your neck is like the tower of David.
> . . . .
> Your two breasts are like two fawns,
>   twins of a gazelle,
>   that feed among the lilies.
>   *(Song of Solomon 4:1c–2, 3b, 4a, 5)*

I can assure you that if that text had more subtlety in its
original context, it was lost on our snickering group!

But perhaps most important, the Bible encourages us to
make laughter and joy a part of our daily lives. The psalmist exhorts us saying, "Be glad in the LORD and rejoice, O
righteous, and shout for joy, all you upright in heart" (Ps.
32:11). And the apostle Paul, writing to the Philippians,
says, "Rejoice in the Lord always; again I will say, Rejoice"
(Phil. 4:4). A healthy faith, the Scriptures seem to suggest,
is also a laughing faith.

So today, give thanks to God for the people in your life
who make you laugh. And give thanks for a God who not
only wants us to laugh but also delights in our rejoicing.

Scripture Readings: Psalm 32:11; Philippians 4:4

For Further Reflection

— Who are the people in your life who regularly make you laugh? Consider thanking them for the joy they infuse in your life.

— Are there parts of the Bible that make you laugh? If so, what are they? If not, why not?

— What are ways that you can bring more laughter to the people whose paths you cross today?

DELIGHT—GOD'S AND OURS

Jesuit Father Gregory Boyle, who has devoted his life
to helping "homies" (gang members in LA) change their
lives, is stretching my edges this morning. I have just finished reading his chapter on "Gladness" in his book *Tattoos
on the Heart*, and it is delightful. He has me laughing out
loud, recounting the best homie excuse for not coming to
work: "I have Anal Blindness . . . I just can't see my ass
coming to work today."* He has me chuckling over the
malapropisms of homies in worship leadership: "A reading from the letter of Paul to the Phillipinos;" confusing
the word *Gentiles* with *genitals* (Fr. Greg swears that if we
will do the same while reading the book of the Acts of the
Apostles, it will liven up the book as never before!).† And
he recounts the story of a homie who was too cool to get
excited by much—until he took biology in high school.
"DAMN, G ["G" is the way the homies address the good
father]—BIOOOLOGY. THAT'S THE BOOOOOMB,
right there. . . . Watcha dog . . . on Monday, we're gonna
DIGEST a frog!"‡

The stories exude the kind of gladness Fr. Greg clearly
finds in his vocation on a daily basis—despite the 168
funerals of young people he has also attended. But the theology of this chapter—that's what gives me pause. For at
its heart is Fr. Greg's belief that God created us to delight
in us and that nothing delights God more than our finding

---

*Gregory Boyle, *Tattoos on the Heart: The Power of Boundless Compassion* (New York:
Free Press, 2010), 148.
†Ibid., 155.
‡Ibid., 154.

delight in the world. As Fr. Greg puts it, "Delighting is
what occupies God, and God's hope is that we join in.
That God's joy may be in us and this joy may be complete.
We just happen to be God's joy. That takes some getting
used to."*

When I reflect on why I have a hard time buying,
whole-cloth, into that theology—much as it appeals to
me—several hindrances come to mind. The first is my
Calvinist upbringing, where the field of delight was usually a very brief pit stop on the way to the more important
lands of obligation and obedience. Yes, it's okay to delight
occasionally in God and God's grace, my church seemed
to teach me, but never ever forget that your greater obligation is to discern God's will and follow it—which always
involves self-sacrifice and denial. That God's will might
actually *be* for me to "delight" in God? Now that's an altogether different proposition.

It's ironic when I think about it, because I also memo-
rized the Westminster Catechism of my church as a child,
and in it the very first question is "What is the chief end of
[humanity]?" And the very first answer is "[Humanity's]
chief end is to worship God *and to enjoy God forever*" (emphasis added). While the worshiping part of that answer was
certainly stressed in the church of my childhood, the enjoying part sometimes got shortchanged. Consequently I grew
up with a strong sense of what I *ought* to do and *should* be
doing, along with a healthy suspicion that if I were enjoying life too much, I probably wasn't pleasing God.

These days I find that same tendency at the liberal
Protestant seminary where I teach. Don't get me wrong.
There is a lot of joy in that place (as indeed there was in
the church of my childhood), and I will forever be grateful
for the ways in which it has restored to me the joy in my

*Ibid., 158.

own vocation. But there is also a strong sense of obligation at its heart—a sense that if we are not doing God's work of justice and peacemaking in the world, we are not living as God would have us live. And sometimes that tendency makes delight just a wee bit suspect.

If I go deeper, I'll have to acknowledge that it's not just the "our chief end is to delight God" part of Fr. Greg's theology that causes me pause; it's also the notion that God created us to delight in us. Really? While that might have been God's original intent, surely things got messed up after sin entered the world. How can we possibly delight God when we consistently get it all wrong?

Father Greg doesn't seem to dwell on that question—despite the fact that he is ministering to young people who have gotten it all wrong time and time again. Rather, he encourages us to look around, in the little humorous and not-so-humorous things that happen to us in the course of an ordinary day, and to find as much delight as possible. He also encourages us to look upon one another, not as people who have "gotten it all wrong" but as people who delight God. He writes, "I suppose Jesus walks into a room and loves what he finds there. Delights in it, in fact. Maybe, He makes a beeline to the outcasts and chooses, in them, to go where love has not yet arrived. His ways aren't our ways, but they sure could be."*

Perhaps it is here—at the intersection of love and delight—that our deepest gladness in God lays. For if we love as deeply as Jesus did and as Fr. Greg does—seeing God's delight in those the world labels "outcasts" and "sinners"—then we are able to more fully experience delight as well.

Scripture Reading: Isaiah 65:18

*Ibid., 155.

For Further Reflection

— Where have you known *delight* this past week in your life's journey?

— Where do you encounter outcasts and sinners in your daily walk, people who might open you anew to the delight God intends for you and for all creation?

— Is it hard for you to believe that God created you to *delight* in God and God's creation? Why or why not?

DEALING WITH FRUSTRATION

Frustration is one of those emotions I don't know how to handle well. And the past few months have been incredibly frustrating. We are trying to sell our house at a seriously depressed price in a lousy market — which has enough challenges of its own. But right at the point when we thought we had committed buyers, they dropped out because, after a heavy rain, we had water accumulating on our garage floor.

Over the past two months I have met with nine different contractors — each with a different opinion regarding what the problem is and how to fix it. Each of these meetings has required me to travel one-hundred-forty miles round-trip and to lose most of a workday. GRRRRRR! We are now on our third "solution" to the problem. The first involved getting an excavator to redo the drainage system under our back deck to make sure that none of the water from the downspouts was causing the problem. No change. The second involved getting a plumber to clear the drainage pipes in the backyard to make sure they are draining well. No change. The last (and most expensive solution by far) involved having dry basement experts dig through the concrete in the back of our garage and install a French drain with a sump pump below the foundation to take out the extra moisture in the soil below the garage. And yes, you guessed it. No change whatsoever. The floor is as wet as ever. And no water was found under the garage.

Meanwhile our realtor has basically refused to show the house until we fix the problem.

What do you do when life deals you frustration — especially over something as inconsequential as a *garage*? I tend to get angry (at the contractors, at the realtor, at the buyers who backed out), defeated ("we will never sell this house; it will be an albatross around our necks forever"), and anxious (waking up at 3:30 a.m. and trying to figure out what to do next). I also tend to replay those tapes of Jesus telling us not to lay up treasures on earth, where moth and rust (and water) corrupt over and over again in my head (see Matt. 6:19). "This is what we get for laying up our treasures on earth," I think to myself, "headache after headache after headache. You are only reaping what you sowed."

But then I think about people I know who have become frustrated over far more consequential things in life: inconclusive test results, chronic pain from which there is no relief, a serious breakdown in the judicial system, the inability—no matter how long and hard a person works— to provide safe and secure housing for family. And I would never say to one of them, "You are only reaping what you sowed."

In times of frustration, Christians often dole out platitudes—to others and to themselves:

"Don't worry. God won't give you more than you can bear."

"Behind every cloud there is a silver lining.

"When life deals you lemons, make lemonade."

"All in God's good timing."

"There must be a purpose in this you can't yet see."

I find such platitudes annoying at best and harmful at worst. Sometimes life simply deals us lemons. Period.

And yet, I also admire those people who take seasons of frustration in their lives and, with God's help, "redeem" them. This past year, I had a long conversation with one of my students, who spent almost two years waiting for a judicial trial that never happened. The person who accused him finally admitted that she had accused him falsely. Two years of his life spent on hold for something he did not do—and that as an African American male who knew that if he had been white and wealthy, the judicial process would have treated him very differently.

Yet when I talked with my student, what moved me deeply was his spirit—especially his lack of bitterness. He names the injustices he encountered boldly and forthrightly. But he has also channeled some of his deep frustrations into his desire to go to law school after completing divinity school and to work with other people of color who are experiencing similar injustices in the criminal justice system. He has found his vocation.

I honestly have no idea what it would mean to "redeem" my experience this summer with our garage—or whether that's even possible. But I do know that platitudes don't help. For now, I pray that I can keep my spirits up and that, eventually, we will find a solution to this seemingly insoluble problem. And if, eventually, I can glimpse something that looks like redemption—or even partial redemption—I will welcome it gladly. Meanwhile, I keep praying for that one buyer for whom a damp garage floor won't pose a major problem.

Scripture Reading: Matthew 6:25–30

For Further Reflection
— For most of us, simply repeating Jesus' challenge to us to "not worry" when frustrations accost us in life is not sufficient. How do you get those words of Jesus to resound not only in your head but also in your spirit?
— When you are anxious and frustrated, what do you find works best for diffusing or relieving those emotions?
— What role might prayer and meditation play in our efforts not to become paralyzed by anxiety?

THREE TRUTHS (PLUS ONE)
ABOUT PRAYER

My mom is a contemporary saint. Everyone in my family thinks so, and when you live with a person for as long as we lived with Mom, you are not fooled. You know.

I once heard my mom's older brother, my Uncle Jim, say that Mom was just born better than everyone else. But I know that's not true. Mom's sainthood has been forged in the crucible of disciplined prayer, steadfast faith, and a heartfelt desire to live her life in service of God and others. She gave her life completely to Christ years ago at a Billy Graham crusade, and she has never taken it back.

Recently, Mom told me that she had learned three things about prayer in her eighty-eight years of life. "Prayer," she said, "requires work. Prayer works. And prayer leads to work." How aptly those three statements sum up my mom's approach to her life in faith.

Prayer requires work. For as long as I can remember—back to my days as a very young child—Mom has gotten up earlier than the rest of our family to pray for us. In my childhood, there was a tiny den off our dining room, which served as Mom's study and prayer room. And we all knew that when she was in there in the early mornings, she was talking with God. To this day, Mom continues to pray for us in the early morning hours—as well as for a host of other people and our broken world.

Mom's prayer life is disciplined. She keeps a prayer journal. She writes down her joys and thanksgivings, as well as her intercessions, and we are all grateful to be on her list. At one stage in her life she used the Lord's Prayer as her guide—adding her own contemporary words after each petition in that ancient prayer. She is ever open to new ways of praying, and at one point she gave me a copy of a prayer for me that she had written out in longhand back in my early adulthood, when I was on the verge of marrying the wrong man. I am convinced to this day that Mom prayed me out of that marriage and also prayed me into the grace-filled marriage that has sustained me now for over four decades.

Mom is our family's personal prayer warrior. Whenever my husband and I confront a crisis in our life, he will laughingly say to me, "Time to call out the big guns. Call your mom and get her praying." The metaphor is terribly mixed. (We are aware that we are inappropriately using militaristic imagery for a saintly act.) But there is something about the prayer of a righteous woman that God evidently does not ignore!

Which leads me to Mom's next affirmation: *Prayer works.* One of the values of keeping a prayer journal, Mom tells me, is that she can go back at the end of a season and look back and realize how many of her prayers have been answered: prayers for healing, prayers for safety, prayers for comfort, prayers for wisdom, prayers for guidance.

My middle brother was estranged from the church for decades. He wanted nothing to do with it. But Mom prayed for him ceaselessly, and about a decade ago, after watching a friend lose a child to suicide and seeing that he had nowhere to turn for solace and comfort, my brother returned to church. He—who lost his job in the recession of 2008 and who barely gets by these days on the money he earns from delivering papers and pizzas—is now a tither and an every Sunday church attender, who recently finished a multiyear term heading the board of an organization that provides transitional housing for alcoholic men in recovery. He is an inspiration to us all.

My youngest brother longed for a family, and so Mom prayed for him. At age fifty, he met Susan, a single mom with a teenage son, via an online dating service. I performed their wedding service a few years ago, and we have all delighted in watching my youngest brother embrace both the joys and the responsibilities of a family after years of bachelorhood.

And Mom's prayers for me have continued to bear fruit as well. She prayed me out of a job that was robbing me of life and spirit, through a bout with cancer that followed, and onto a new vocational path that has been fulfilling and rewarding and deeply satisfying. That she also prays for our children and grandchildren is a great comfort to me.

Mom does not have much patience with the kind of theology that encourages us to treat God like a magic genie who is simply waiting around to do our bidding. Nor does she believe that people of faith have a greater claim on God's mercy than do others. Hers is a far more humble approach to prayer. It is founded on the belief that when we live in relationship with God, we talk to God about everything that is going on in our lives, and we lay all our wants and desires at the throne of God's grace, knowing that God knows what is best for us. She goes back through her prayer journal each year not to prove that God answers prayers (she already knows that) but so that she can be sure to express appropriate gratitude for those answers.

Finally, *prayer leads to work*. For Mom, prayer is not simply a practice through which we meet God and lay our burdens on God. Prayer is also the place where God speaks to us and calls us to new ventures in service and mission. Some of my mom's best ideas are forged in the crucible of prayer. One example is the "Christmas Share" program at her church, which started with Mom's concern for the poor in her larger community; it now funnels thousands of dollars each year from excessive Christmas gifts for family and friends into donations given in their honor for worthy causes. It is also in prayer that she senses the prodding of the Spirit to visit a friend who is going through a tough time, to call one of us children and let us know she is thinking of us, or to propose a new idea for the worship life of her retirement community. It is appropriate that, for Mom, prayer comes at the beginning of her day, because, if truth be told, it is out of prayer that the rest of her day flows in obedience to the guidance she receives there.

If I were to add a fourth truth about prayer I have come to know from observing Mom's prayer life, it would be this: *Prayer works on us.* Through the years, this ordinary woman of faith has become an extraordinary saint of God. She wasn't born better than the rest of us. But through the Spirit's work in and through her prayer life, she has become what God intends us all to be: a saint.

Scripture Reading: 1 Thessalonians 5:16–22

For Further Reflection
— Who are some of the best pray-ers in your life, and how do you see the fruit of their faithfulness in prayer reflected in the lives they live?
— Reflect on your own prayer life. Which of the four affirmations about prayer rings most true for you?
— If you are in need of a more disciplined prayer life, what are the tools and practices that could make prayer a regular activity for you? Are you willing to take on one or more of these as a new discipline in faith?

SIMPLE PLEASURES

Each morning, I start my day by writing down my thanks-givings to God in my prayer journal. It is a practice I first learned from my mother (who still begins her mornings in this manner at age eighty-eight), though I was well into midlife before it became second nature to me. It is a practice that I sometimes share with my young granddaughters when they are visiting—asking them to tell me what they are especially thankful for and adding their words to my own.

This morning, I am on my second day of vacation with family, at a lake in Maine. It is early yet in this peaceful place, where the sun glints through the tall trees and the mist rises over the waters. I am the only person awake, and as I write down this morning's list, I am struck by how much joy I find in life's simple pleasures:

> Thank you, O God,
> For the gift of being on vacation in this beautiful place;
> For swimming with Maddie (age 5) and Bryn (age 3), and
> seeing their delight in buoyancy and water and family
> splashing about together;
> For Alison and Maddie (mother and daughter) riding on
> the tube together behind PopPop's boat, and for holding
> dear little Bryn close in my lap as we watched them
> enjoy their ride;
> For "Miss Ethel" (my husband's deceased mother) and for
> the vision we had yesterday of her sitting on the motor
> boat we have named in her honor—cup of coffee in one
> hand and cigarette in the other—and delighting in all the
> fun around her;

For all seven of us children and adults playing a rollicking
    game of Uno together, followed by dinner by candlelight
    on the back deck;
For meatloaf and ice cream, for fresh green beans and new
    potatoes, for cooked apples and margaritas, for Uncle
    Jimmy's iced tea;
For no-mind novels, and for the love of my man;
For mist on the water and singing "Old MacDonald"
    around the campfire;
For the gift of this week apart together.

The older I get, the more I realize how much it is the
simple, incarnational pleasures in life that grace it with joy
and delight. God became flesh and blessed flesh with holiness so that we might see the holy in the ordinary as well.
When we do so, I think it makes God smile. Food and fire,
trees and water, games and singing, sex and sun, children
and aging adults—all are gifts of a benevolent Creator who
delighted the first time the Spirit blew over the waters and
fashioned this world and us earth creatures from nothing and who delights all over again when we revel in the
beauty and glory of the world around us.

So let us praise the God of simple pleasures. That is
certainly what the psalmists of old did. They blessed the
God who made

> fire and hail, snow and frost,
>   stormy wind fulfilling his command!
> Mountains and all hills,
>   fruit trees and all cedars!
> Wild animals and all cattle,
>   creeping things and flying birds!"
>   (Ps. 148:8–10)

And let us not forget that the God who created flesh and

matter and creeping things and flying birds blessed them all and called them "very good."

Scripture Reading: Psalm 148

For Further Reflection
— Make a list of the "simple pleasures" for which you are most grateful this day.

PRAYING FOR RAIN

I once had a theology professor whose favorite question of new students was, "Is it appropriate to pray for rain?" For him, the question was a way of pressing us to think more carefully about what we believed about God and about prayer. Did we believe in a God who had set the natural forces of the universe in order and who then left them to run according to their own natural laws? Or did we believe in a God who might intervene in the natural order of nature to answer a prayer? And if we believed in the former, why bother to pray for rain?

When I graduated from seminary and went to my first parish, one of the very first prayer requests I received during Sunday morning worship was from a dairy farmer who asked me to pray for rain. "Our wells are running dry," he said, "and if this drought keeps up we will have no grain to feed our cattle this winter. Please, Pastor, pray for rain." In that agrarian setting—where life and its sustenance were completely dependent on God's heavenly watering cycle—praying for rain was not a theological parlor game; it was a routine part of faithful worship.

If prayer is about opening our lives—our fears, our hopes, our desires—to the life and purposes of God, if prayer is about living in an honest and open and ever-deepening relationship with the Creator and Sustainer of the universe, then of course we pray for rain. Talking with God about the need for rain is as natural as a child talking to a parent about the need for daily bread. God loves us, God wants us to have what we need for life, and God urges us to pray and make known our needs—whatever they are—to God.

Besides, I have seen enough of life—and of miracles—to realize that there is a thin line in this world between "natural" and "supernatural" occurrences. While I find great comfort in knowing that God ordinarily works in natural and fairly predictable ways, I also find comfort in knowing that God is God and can do anything God chooses—as long as those acts are consistence with God's own loving, merciful being.

Yet it seems to me that this praying for rain question is still a complicated one—not so much because of the nature of God but because of the nature of us human beings. In recent years, many parts of our nation and our world have been undergoing serious droughts caused by global warming. Wells are running dry, not because God has withheld rain, but because humans have wasted, squandered, and polluted the bountiful waters God has given us. To quote that well-known prayer of confession from the *Book of Common Prayer*, "We have left undone those things which we ought to have done, and we have done those things which we ought not to have done." So my question is: do we have any *right* to ask God for more rain? Do we, who have so carelessly, recklessly, and selfishly abused the good gifts God has given, have any right at all to ask for more of the same?

Probably not—unless our prayers for more rain are also coupled with prayers of confession and with deeds that signal our intent to repent of our past actions (and inactions), to turn around, and to respond in a new way toward the precious gift of water with which we have been entrusted. To pray such prayers without giving more vigilant attention to environmental policies, to water conservation, and to our own wasteful water usage (overly long showers, running kitchen faucets, extended lawn watering) is like asking God for daily bread when we are taking it out the backdoor by truckloads and dumping it over cliffs. It is not only the height of audacity and carelessness; it is also insulting to God and to the others who share this planet with us.

Yet I also take heart that prayer in the Bible seems to be more about our desiring than our deserving, and more about God's mercy than about God's just judging. "Is there anyone among you who, if your child asks for bread, will give a stone?" asked Jesus (Matt. 7:9). "Ask, and it will be given you; search, and you will find; knock, and the door will be opened for you" (v. 7). So while I know we don't deserve any more water, I pray nonetheless—hoping that my prayers, coupled with at least a few signs of a repentant spirit, will be a pleasing offering unto the God who (thankfully) has been known in the past to send rain on the just *and* the unjust.

This week—in the midst of a severe drought in our state—it rained for forty-eight solid hours: a gentle, steady rain that allowed the thirsty earth plenty of time to drink its welcome waters. By the end of the second day, weather reporters told us that we had received three full inches of the precious liquid. Through my own backyard well, I feel far more connected these days to those dairy farmers in my first parish and to their prayers for rain. And so when rain comes, as it did this week, I thank God for every undeserved drop.

Scripture Reading: Matthew 7:7–11

For Further Reflection
— Reflect on water and the role it plays in your life. Pause to thank God for all the things water makes possible in your life.
— Are there areas in which you need to repent of wastefulness regarding water?

— What changes in attitudes or actions might repentance require of you?
— How might you do your part to advocate and work for the conservation and care of our water resources?

KEEPING IT SIMPLE

My clergy spouse and I attend a lot of weddings. And frankly, I am appalled at the amount of money people spend on weddings. At one wedding I attended this year, I know the price tag for the family was well over half a million dollars. Half a million dollars for a wedding and a reception where the focus is supposed to be on the ritual act itself—the marrying of the bride and groom—and not on the flowers, the food and drink, or the band.

I understand that people like to throw a good party for their friends to celebrate marriages. And I'm all for a celebration to mark this important rite of passage in the lives of two people who are pledging their troth to one another. But from time to time, I am reminded of how simple a wedding and a reception can be, and both still be beautiful and also deeply meaningful.

One of the most memorable weddings I attended was of two seminarians who were students of mine twenty years ago. The wedding was held at an inner-city church in a troubled neighborhood, where we were greeted and welcomed by members of their church youth group. The service was focused not just on the couple but also on their calling to work for justice and peace in the world. I remember that one of the Scripture texts read was the one about righteousness and peace kissing (Ps. 85:10). Instead of being walked down the aisle by their parents, this bride and groom walked down the dual aisles on opposite sides, smiling at one another over the congregants. Both bride and groom had a circle of flowers in their hair and were dressed simply yet beautifully. Each of them had attendants that were both male and female.

One of the most striking things about their wedding was how many people were involved in contributing something to their celebration. A friend of the couple wrote a song that he sang from the piano as a part of their service. An artist friend designed their invitations and also the large poster we all signed with our good wishes as we entered the sanctuary. (We were told it would be framed and hung in a place of honor in their home.) Another friend, who had at one time worked as a caterer, took charge of the food for the reception—arranging the bountiful loaves of bread many hands had made, the various cheeses, and the delicious salads the couple had purchased for their vegetarian feast, in an artful display. And still others proffered their gifts through toasts and prayers for the couple. Instead of buying wedding gifts, all of us guests were encouraged to make contributions to Habitat for Humanity, to help establish homes for others, in honor of the new home that was being established through this wedding.

This wedding was as beautiful as any I've ever attended, and people had a wonderful, celebratory time. But it was also simple. And somehow that very simplicity focused our attention on what was at the heart of it all: the joining in marriage of these two people who loved one another and who were pledging to live their lives in holy union and in service to God.

In the story of Mary and Martha in the Bible, the one in which they host Jesus for a meal in their home, Jesus turns to Martha and says, "Martha, Martha, you are worried and distracted by many things; there is need of only one thing" (Luke 10:41–42a). Martha has been working hard in the kitchen to prepare a meal for him, and she is frustrated that her sister Mary has been sitting at Jesus' feet and learning from him instead of helping her. I remember years ago reading a commentator who suggested that what Jesus might have been saying is: "Martha, you are going to all this trouble to fix a huge meal for me. But a one-dish meal would have been sufficient."

That line came back to me at another wedding reception I attended last night. This wedding, too, was simpler and more economical than most I attend. Instead of multiple options for dinner entrees, we were served one dish—a chicken dish (with a vegetarian option for those who don't eat meat). Instead of an open bar throughout the reception, the couple opted for a cash bar (which cut down significantly on drinking). Instead of a band, they had hired a DJ. It was all we needed. Indeed, I found that a simpler feast allowed us all to focus more on the wedding couple, to celebrate them and their lives, and to give thanks for that which was at the heart of this event: their union under God.

Scripture Reading: Luke 10:38–42

For Further Reflection
— Think of a celebration you have attended that was festive yet also simple.
— What did you appreciate most about it?
— What did you learn from that experience about possibilities for celebrating significant life events with simplicity?
— In what ways are you most like Mary in this biblical story? In what ways like Martha? What do you learn from each of them and Jesus' interaction with them?

KEEPING SABBATH

For as long as I can remember, Sundays have had a different rhythm in my life than other days of the week. When I was a child, my parents were strict observers of Sunday as a day set apart, a Christian "Sabbath" day. Going to Sunday school and church was not optional for us; it was required. So my three brothers and I all got dressed up, piled in the family car, and off we went.

Sunday dinner, shared around the dining room table after we got home from church, was a family affair, with three generations present. There was even a formula for the meal itself: roast beef, rice and gravy (we were southerners, after all), little green peas, and salad of some variety. Occasionally, there were also hot, homemade rolls.

My mother believed that people shouldn't be made to work on Sunday (people other than her, that is), so we did not eat in restaurants on Sundays. Nor did we children do homework. I still remember being mortified in the eighth grade when my mother sent a note to my history teacher saying that an assigned project would be late because our family observed Sunday as a Sabbath and that she had made me go to bed at midnight on Saturday night before the assignment was complete. The note itself wasn't mortifying; it was that the teacher was so enamored with the novelty of it that she read it aloud in front of the entire class. Ouch! It's one thing to be different; it's another to be publicly called out as different in adolescence.

Since we children were not allowed to ride bikes or go to the beach on Sundays (we lived only twenty minutes from the ocean), we spent Sunday afternoons playing

Bible Bee and Bible Lotto. Our mom usually took a nap at some point. And frankly, I remember Sunday afternoons in my childhood as being rather boring and devoid of fun (though I became thankful for those Bible trivia games when it came to passing the Bible content ordination exam in seminary!)

A lot has changed in the last fifty years—including my own observance of a Sabbath day. But Sundays still have a rhythm all their own, some of which echo the best of childhood rhythms. I sleep a bit later, linger longer over my coffee and journaling, and try to avoid work that is uncreative or that weighs me down. I go to church; I miss it if I don't. After a simple lunch together, my husband and I often spend the afternoon going for a walk or a drive—followed by a good, long nap.

While I know it is not possible for everyone to have such a Sabbath day on Sunday (indeed, for many years when I was engaged in parish ministry, Sunday was a major workday for me), I do think the Hebrew people were onto something with their notion of setting a day apart for God, and for the rest and renewal we so desperately need to give our lives balance and wholeness. Human beings were not made to work seven days a week. According to Genesis, even God took a day off when creating the world! And we *were* created for the worship and praise of God. As Saint Augustine put it so well, "Our hearts are restless until they find their rest in Thee."

As I observe modern individuals and families, I think they often get half of this equation right. They know that it's important to spend time on Sunday doing fun things and relaxing. But they often miss out on the other half. This is God's day. And to be truly renewed, we not only need time apart but also need time apart *with God*.

Rabbi Abraham Heschel has referred to Sabbath as

a sanctuary in time that hallows all other time.* There is something profoundly true about this insight. I am grateful both for the sanctuary aspect of Sabbath and for the way in which incorporating observance of this day into the rhythm of our weeks also helps to hallow all our other days.

Sabbath, at its best, is a gift, not a burden. It deserves to be hallowed — not only for God's sake but also for our own.

Scripture Reading: Exodus 20:8–11

For Further Reflection
— Think about your Sabbath observance (or lack thereof). What happens to you in life when you fail to observe a day for rest, renewal, and worship?
— What happens to you in life when you do observe such a day?
— How might you make your Sabbath observance more regular and more meaningful? What small steps might you take this week toward that end?

*See Abraham Joshua Heschel, *The Sabbath* (New York: Farrar, Straus and Giroux, 1951).

A TASTE OF HOME

As a transplanted southerner living in the northeastern
part of the United States, there are certain foods that I
miss. One of them is vinegar-based pork barbecue. (My
husband and I always head immediately for a BBQ place
when we go to North Carolina to visit extended family.)
Another is grits. (Yes, I know we southerners are teased
about them, but many of us genuinely love them.) And a
third is pimento cheese. (If you don't know what this is,
you have my sympathies.)

I still recall going to a birthday party in New York City
some years ago, where everybody brought food to add to
the table, and heading directly for what looked, for all the
world, like a container of pimento cheese. I was elated to
find this delicacy in the northland, and I couldn't wait to
learn where you could purchase it in New York. Alas, I
soon discovered that the container did not hold pimento
cheese after all. It was hummus. The same color, but the
consistency was all wrong. To say that I was disappointed
would be an understatement.

Imagine my delight, then, when last week, as I was doing
my routine grocery shopping in my Connecticut super-
market, I unexpectedly ran across a container of pimento
cheese (labeled "Palmetto Cheese")! Suspicious at first, I
looked immediately to see where it had been made. And
when I saw that it came from Pawley's Island, South Carolina, I knew I was home free.

Pimento cheese tastes like home to me. In fact, there is
nothing quite as delightful on a summer's day as a pimento
cheese sandwich with large juicy slabs of fresh garden
tomatoes on top. Yum! One bite and I am transported

to another time and another place and to fond memories of my family of origin—where there was always a tub of pimento cheese in the refrigerator on family vacations.

For many church people I know, the bread and wine of the Lord's Supper also taste like "home"—our home in God and with God's large, extended family. I remember a time almost forty years ago when my husband and I were strangers in the land of South Korea, teaching English and theology in a seminary there and living in a small apartment in a dormitory on the seminary campus. We didn't speak much of the language yet. The customs were all new to us. And our American homes seemed very far away indeed in that pre-Skype era. We went to the opening-of-the-academic-year chapel service at the seminary, and again, much of it was completely unfamiliar. Aside from a few evangelical hymns, whose tunes we knew from our childhood, we were pretty lost in the service— until, that is, it came time for Communion. As the ushers passed the bread and juice down the pews where we were seated, we finally tasted something familiar, something comforting, something that spoke "home" to us. But this time it was a much larger and more inclusive home than the one we had left behind.

I suspect that Jesus knew his disciples were going to need a taste of home after he left this earth, and that is part of why he instituted the Lord's Supper. Growing up as Jews in Palestine, the disciples had known the elements of bread and wine their whole lives. But as Jesus ate his last meal with them—one that some Gospel writers indicate was the Passover meal—he imbued it with new meaning. "Take, eat; this is *my body*. . . this is *my blood* of the covenant, which is poured out for many for the forgiveness of sins"; "Do this in remembrance of *me*" (Matt. 26:26c, 28; Luke 22:19c, emphasis added).

A friend of mine recently lost her husband after only

eight years of marriage. She had waited all her life to find this man, and losing him has been almost more than she can bear. She told me recently that even going to church is difficult—because the Episcopal church she attends is the one where her husband grew up. She said that going forward for Communion is especially painful.

But she keeps going back. And I'm guessing that, in part, it's because she knows—deep down inside—that this is one of those places where she can draw close to this man she dearly loves. One of those places where she can still share a meal with him. One of those places where she can also imagine that one day they will be together again—in a home that knows no earthly bounds.

Scripture Reading: Matthew 26:26–30

For Further Reflection
— What foods taste like "home" to you, and what images and emotions do they bring to mind?
— Have you ever experienced the Lord's Supper as "food from home"? If so, what is it about that meal that makes it home-like for you?

THE GIFT OF FRIENDSHIP AND FAMILY

(WRITTEN AT AGES 60–64)

THE WIDOWS

The Bible says a lot about our need as Christians to care for widows and orphans, and I confess that in my own thinking I have tended to group the widows in with a whole lot of other people the Scriptures view as being "the least of these"—the poor, the hungry, and the dispossessed—and have not given them a lot of thought.

Lately, though, my perspective has been changing. It all started with a sermon I heard one of my students preach, in which she talked about the widows in the congregation where she is doing an internship, as well as the widows in her own personal life, and how strong and wise and resilient they are.[*] She talked about widows running businesses, buying and selling property, organizing charity events, and serving on various boards in the church and the community. She talked about the wisdom they share from their years of lived experience and about the faith that sustains them in good times and bad. She talked about the various ways in which they serve their local churches and communities and about the many gifts they bring to that service.

As I listened to her sermon, I found myself nodding and thinking, "Yes, these are the widows I know and love in my own life and in my congregation as well." They are women of resilience and strength and talent. They are people of faith and perseverance and insight. Though all of them have suffered one of the most heart-wrenching losses a human being can suffer—the death of a beloved

---

[*]Sarah Godbehere preached this sermon in the "Principles and Practices of Preaching" course at Yale Divinity School on September 20, 2012.

spouse—they are digging deep into the resources of their faith and finding ways to survive and even thrive. They are reinventing their lives with imagination and courage. They are forming communities of support for and with one another. And in the process, they are giving witness to that which is at the very heart of our faith: a belief in life after death, in joy that flows out of deep sorrow, and in community that is forged through shared pain and suffering.

Several years ago, when my husband became pastor of the congregation where we currently worship, he was met with an onslaught of deaths. Three leading men in the church and the community died within his first few months on the job, and our community mourned their passing. But their widows—Patty, Jane, and Gill—lived on. I am inspired by how they do so. They all attend the same worship service (the early service) each Sunday morning, where they check to make sure each is properly situated in her own pew. After the service they, along with assorted other friends and church members, take over a local coffee shop where they debrief the service and sermon, catch up with one another, and continue the communion begun in worship. All of them serve the church in a variety of ways—on the altar guild, the stewardship committee, the flower guild, the vestry.

One of these women and her husband—both of them justices of the peace—performed many weddings together before his death, and she told me recently that she will soon be officiating at the wedding of her granddaughter. Another continues the foundation work her husband began, traveling the country to promote a cause they both believed in. Yet another serves on various non-profit boards. This past year she courageously sold the home in which she and her husband had lived and shared memories for decades, and she moved into a smaller place closer to town.

If truth be told, these widows, along with others, now

form something of a guild in our church. When another woman in our church lost her husband unexpectedly last year, they were the ones who were there for her, immediately—knowing far better than the rest of us what she was going through and what she most needed.

While the Bible frequently refers to widows as a group, widows play a major role in several stories. I think, for instance, of the Widow of Zarephath, who welcomed the prophet Elijah into her home during a time of severe famine, prepared food for him with the last bit of meal she possessed, and whose hospitable faith was rewarded with a never-ending supply of meal (1 Kgs. 17:8–16). I think of the widow Anna, who served as a prophet in the temple in Jerusalem when Jesus was born and who—along with the aged Simeon—praised God mightily when Mary and Joseph presented their child (Luke 2:36–38). And I think of the widow that Jesus lifted up for his disciples as an example of sacrificial giving; the one whose gift of two copper coins was more prized than all others because "she out of her poverty has put in all she had to live on" (Luke 21:4b). Widows, in Jesus' time, as in ours, were faithful servants of God, who lived out their vocations in a variety of ways.

Several years ago, my beloved husband of many years had a health scare, and I contemplated for a few weeks the possibility of becoming a widow. The prospect terrified me. He is my soul mate, my partner, my lover, and my dearest friend; and the thought of going on without him was more than I could bear. I knew that if he died, all I would want to do was die with him.

But should, God forbid, I lose him in this life, I hope and pray the widows will be there for me: surrounding me with their cloak of empathy and understanding; sustaining me with their kindness and care; reminding me that life can and does go on and that with God's help, I can too.

Scripture Reading: Luke 2:36–38

For Further Reflection
— Think about the widows you know. Name the traits that come to mind when you think of them.
— What do they teach you about living and persevering in the face of death?

MOTHER, LOVER, FRIEND

In her book *Models of God*, theologian Sallie McFague talks about God as Mother, Lover, and Friend. At first, some of those images didn't mean much to me. Or rather, I wouldn't let them get close enough to mean much to me. I liked the Mother image. That implied a female God. But the Lover and Friend images seemed to reduce God too much to human level for my liking, turning God into some kind of cosmic buddy and robbing God of traits I depend on, like sovereignty and righteousness and the power to do something about evil and injustice in the world.

This morning, as I was reading sections from *The Showings of Julian of Norwich*—where she speaks of Jesus as a mother who nourishes us with the food of his own body and of God as Mother, full of wisdom, who reforms and restores us—I contemplated anew what it would mean to embrace God as Mother. Julian and other mystics like her who focus on God's abundant, merciful love for us also appear to have the capacity to love God more than I do and sometimes make me feel deficient in faith. If I'm honest with myself, I'm not sure I always love God sufficiently. I respect God. I depend on God. I want to please God. I am very glad that God is God. But love? Somehow it's hard for me to love this amorphous being who is so powerful and all-knowing and capable of restoring all things to justice and righteousness.

It dawned on me this morning, though, that whether or not I love God depends a lot on how I imagine God. When I imagine God as a mother or grandmother—a woman with a full bosom, a comfortable, well-padded lap, and large arms always ready to welcome, encircle, rock, and hold me close—my capacity for loving God also increases.

And that's when I started thinking about other images that could help me love God more. Who could I imagine God as being like (except on a much grander scale) that would engender not just my fear, my respect, my awe, and my trust—but also my love.

The image that first came to mind was that of my husband—a man who has a remarkable sixth sense about knowing who people are, figuring out what they need, and loving them unconditionally. I often feel with him that I am as close to the genuine article of love as I'll ever get in this life. "I can deal with a male God," I thought, "if God is like my beloved spouse."

But something didn't ring true about that. It's not his maleness that's the issue here. It's compassion: the compassion of a gentle, kind, considerate, passionate lover who knows me better than I know myself and who (remarkably) still loves me completely. If God is like that, then, oh, how good God is! If God is like that, then, oh, how I adore God who is life to me.

And that's when I also started thinking of friends. The women friends with whom I have wept and rejoiced, prayed and played. The male friends with whom I have worked and laughed, taught and learned. God is like them, I thought. And that means God is good.

But more than that, if I think of God as Mother, Lover, and Friend, God becomes loveable. Not loveable like a puppy; loveable like a wise mother who always knows when to speak and when to be silent, when to hold close and heal, and when to gently nudge toward new ventures in faith. Loveable like a life partner who waits at the end of the day with arms outstretched, a smile framing his beautiful face. Loveable like a friend who knows just what word of encouragement is needed—and when. A friend I know will be there for me in the darkest hours of my soul.

God is like that—and more. And maybe, just maybe, if I start reimaging God, I can also love God more.

Scripture Reading: Mark 12:28–31

For Further Reflection

— What images of God will allow you to love God more fully, and to receive with open arms God's love for you?

SAVE ME FROM
A STUPID LIFE

In her poem "Poet's Progress," Lorna Dee Cervantes writes:

> Save me from a stupid life! I prayed.
> Leave me anything but a stupid life."*

Despite her mother's discouragement of Cervantes as a girl — telling her that no one would ever pay her to write so she should become the best maid she could be — Cervantes relentlessly pursued her first love of poetry. She says that pursuit literally saved her life. Right after her first book was published, when she was only twenty-four years old, she looked at a photo of her middle-school class and realized that a full 50 percent of them were dead from the kind of violence that robs too many urban youth of their lives. "I could have been one of them," she writes. In finding her vocation as a poet, she says, I found "the exact opposite of a stupid life."†

I suspect that for many people, whether or not we live "stupid lives" has a lot to do with choices we make — many of them at a very early age. How young we are when we first have to decide how we will answer weighty questions, such as:

— What do I believe about war? Would I fight for my country if drafted to do so? Is there any cause worth dying for? Worth killing for?

*Lorna Dee Cervantes, "Poet's Progress," copyright 1997 by Lorna Dee Cervantes. As quoted in Bill Moyers, *Fooling with Words: A Celebration of Poets and Their Craft* (New York: William Morrow and Co., 1999), 44.
†Cervantes tells this story in Moyers, *Fooling with Words*, 34–45.

130

— What do I believe about money and its role in my life? How many "things" will I need to be happy and free of anxiety? What relationship do I see between my financial well-being and that of the rest of the world?
— What do I believe about family? Do I feel called to share my life with a partner, and if so, what kind of partner? What are the core values I hold dear that my partner must share if we are to live happily and at peace together?
— What will my vocational direction be? Where is the meeting point between "my deep gladness and the world's deep hunger" (as Frederick Buechner defines "vocation"*)?

Because we adults at midlife have lived long enough to know how critical these choices are for shaping our own future's trajectory, it is especially scary to give our children freedom to make choices for themselves. We want to protect them from our pain, our heartaches, always remembering the roads not taken in our own lives—and the difference (for good or ill) taking another route might have made.

At our worst, we pressure our children—in subtle and not-so-subtle ways—to make the same choices we did, forgetting that their individuality might require very different choices for their well-being. I remember my dismay some years ago when I watched the father of one of our children's friends pressure him to go to a college where he could major in business (the father's vocation), when the passion of the son's heart was making music. I know the father did this because he loved his son and feared for his financial security in the future. But I can't help wonder

*Frederick Buechner, *Wishful Thinking: A Seeker's ABC*, revised edition (HarperSan-Francisco, 1993), 119.

what difference it might have made if the son had been allowed to follow his own dream and go to the music school, where he had also been accepted?

I, too, am guilty of trying to make my children in my own image. I remember the catch-up lunch my son, Will, and I had when he was a college freshman. I was expressing concern about some of his recent decisions when he leaned across the table, looked me in the eye, and said, "Mom, it's my life. And these are my choices. I'm a man now, and I'm the one who's going to have to live with them."

He was right. Much as I hate to admit it, he was absolutely right. I have always tried to live by my mother's wise adage, "Our children are only ours for a season—gifts on loan by the God to whom they ultimately belong." But, as parents, it is hard to accept the fact that childhood has ended, that adulthood has begun, and that it is time to give our children back to God.

I still remember the day my mother announced that the time had come for her to do so. I was a college student, and I had been bucking as hard as I could against her guidance, asserting my independence in wise and not-so-wise ways. We were in the kitchen, and I was taking her on about some current piece of advice she was sharing with me that I didn't deem to be wise at all. As I was bracing for the argument I knew would follow, my mother startled me by turning to me calmly and announcing, "Nora, I've been thinking a lot about this, and I have something to say to you. You are an adult now, and you are in God's hands. I have been your mother thus far in your life, guiding your decisions and your decision making. But now it is up to you. Your choices are your choices. I will pray for you. I will still offer you my wisdom. But what you do from now on is up to you. I am cutting you loose to be the adult you are now becoming."

I wish I could say that I was delighted when she made

this announcement, but in truth I was terrified. "No!" I inwardly cried. "Don't cast me out onto the perilous waters of adulthood on my own. I'd much rather thrash about in the water, blaming you for whether I sink or swim, than take responsibility for my own actions." But cut me loose she did. Not to sink or swim on my own, but to be tethered to the umbilical cord of a Mother God who gave me life and birth, and in whose arms I would always be surrounded with infinite wisdom, compassion, and care.

If there is a time to be hypervigilant in prayer, it is when our children are young teenagers and young adults, making all those weighty decisions that literally can mean life or death for them. And if you ask me, Cervantes' prayer is not a bad one to say on a daily basis, "Save him, save her," we plead with God, "from a stupid life."

Scripture Reading: Luke 2:41–52

For Further Reflection
— When he was only twelve years old, Jesus asserted his independence from his earthly parents. What do you think was hardest for Mary and Joseph about Jesus claiming his place in the temple at such a young age?
— What path might they have wanted their son to follow?
— What is it that makes a life "stupid" or not?

FAMILY TIES

(Written at Age 50)

This past weekend, our daughter, twenty-one years young, loaded up a Ryder truck with most of her worldly possessions—including her bed and several other pieces of furniture from her bedroom—and drove from New Jersey to North Carolina, where she will be sharing a house with friends this coming year. Helping her prepare for this journey was a family project, and actually a fun one, as we all shared in her excitement about moving into a place of her own. But when the time actually came for her to depart, there were tears in her eyes. "I'm just sad about leaving my home," she said. And with those words she unleashed all the pent-up mourning I had been trying to hold inside. "I know," I said, hugging her and weeping with her.

We both know that our house will never be home in the same way to her again. She is a woman now, with a life and purpose of her own, and it is time for her to move out and move on. But it's still hard for both of us to cut the umbilical cord that has tethered her to us and to our sacred family space for these past twenty-one years.

As I watched my oldest child and only daughter climb into the cab of the yellow truck yesterday morning, I flashed back thirty years to a summer's day on which I loaded my newly purchased and very-used green Ford Pinto (one of the great lemon cars of all time) with all my worldly possessions and headed off for my first job. What a sense of adventure it was to be charting off—like the pioneer women of old—to a new territory and new life! But I also found myself wondering, as I went up to my daughter's room yesterday morning and wept over its emptiness, if my mother before me had done the same.

It's no wonder that people have such a hard time after death, getting rid of the clothes of their loved ones. And it's no wonder that the Catholic Church for centuries has built cathedrals around sacred relics of Jesus and Mary. We all long for some tangible thing that signifies for us the presence of our loved ones after they are gone—even if only to North Carolina.

But we also know that there are times in life when we cannot cling to our loved ones, just as Jesus' family could not cling to him when he went about God's business. *Family*, as defined in gospel terms, is always much bigger and broader than family of origin. And Jesus was always pressing his family of origin to acknowledge that when he went about doing God's work—healing the sick, eating with outcasts, and bringing good news to those in despair—he was at home.

I have long sympathized with Mary in the story from Mark's Gospel, where she and Jesus' brothers send word to Jesus that they would like some time with him in the midst of his busy schedule. It seems a highly reasonable request, especially given how busy and absent from his home of origin Jesus has been. And yet Jesus does not rush out to hug and welcome and reassure his mother. Instead, he turns to those gathered around him and says, "Here are my mother and my brothers! Whoever does the will of God is my brother and sister and mother" (Mark 3:34–35).

My daughter will be spending her summer working in "Higher Ground," a "safe house" for people with AIDS. Over lunch each day she will commune with members of her newly extended family, as she breaks bread with Jesus and his HIV-positive friends. She started volunteering there this past winter and already has many moving stories to tell of the courage, humor, and faith she has witnessed these past few months.

Like Mary, I'm sure there will be days when I wish that she still lived safely here with us. But deep in my heart, I know the truth; she, like Jesus before her, must be about God's business, and when she is with Jesus and friends, she *is* at home.

"I can't wait for you and Poppa to come see me this summer, Momma," my eldest said yesterday morning, as she prepared to drive her truck out of our driveway. "I can't wait for you to see my house and eat fresh vegetables out of my garden, and have lunch with me at Higher Ground. Will you say the blessing before the meal when you come?"

"Yes," I replied, knowing deep inside that when she welcomes her father, her brother, and me into her newly extended family, the blessings will all be ours.

Scripture Reading: Mark 3:31–35

For Further Reflection
— Reflect on the term *family* and what it means in your life.
— How does Jesus' expanded notion of family help you see it in a new light?
— Where have you been graced with family that extends beyond your blood lines?
— What is graceful in Jesus' teaching about family? What is difficult about it?

IT'S ALL ABOUT TRUST

"It's all about trust." That's what my dear husband said to me yesterday after he spent an hour in the waters of Long Island Sound helping our four-year-old granddaughter Maddie grow more confident in her own water skills.

It was a beach day for our family, in the small seaside town where we now reside. We were spread out on the sand, with an umbrella to provide some shade, a cooler full of sandwiches and drinks for sustenance, and a large mesh bag full of colorful plastic toys. For the first thirty minutes, the two "grandgirls" stayed close to the shore, wetting their feet, but not much else. And then our son, Will, dove into the cold water, swam out to a floating dock, and did a cannonball off it. When he came up grinning, our two-year-old granddaughter Bryn, who was sitting with her mom on the shore, immediately started shaking with excitement, begging that she be allowed to "swim" too. So her dad took her out into the water, and in no time she was scooping and kicking in a circle on her belly as Will held her small frame aloft.

And that's when Maddie decided she wanted to try swimming too. So Pop Pop took her out, and a series of photos I took of the two of them give evidence of her metamorphosis. In the first photo, she is clinging tightly to her grandfather's neck as he gradually takes her out deeper and deeper into the sea. In subsequent pictures, she is holding onto his hands, facing him in the water, and laughing gleefully. And in the final photo, she is standing on her own two feet, chest high in the water, jumping the gentle waves, her own two hands held high in victory.

What a gift it is to watch a child learn to trust the water

and herself in it. Through gentle words of encouragement, a slow but steady metamorphosis takes place. Fear begins to melt away, and new trust, new freedom is born.

I imagine that's how it was with Jesus and Peter as well. It was all about trust. Peter, fearful and anxious in a boat, is tossed about in the stormy sea. Jesus comes to him out of the turbulence, walking calmly across the water and modeling a new way of being. Then Jesus speaks gentle words of assurance to Peter and the other disciples, "Take heart, it is I; do not be afraid" (Matt. 14:27). Finally, Peter undergoes a metamorphosis of his own and starts walking across the sea to meet his Lord.

For some reason, we tend to focus in this text on either the miracle of Jesus walking on the water (where silly jokes abound) or that juncture at which Peter begins to doubt his sea legs and slips deeper into the waters. I prefer to focus on the miracle of Peter's metamorphosis. For a brief moment in time, Peter knows what it is to trust Jesus. And that trust in Jesus allows him to walk confidently in the storm without being engulfed by fear and anxiety in the midst of its chaos.

The reality is that trust in our lives is both a fleeting thing and a growing thing. In fits and starts, we learn to trust God and to know that God is trustworthy. And in the process, we also learn to trust ourselves to God. What I love about the ending of this story is that when Peter begins to sink and cries out, "Lord, save me!" Jesus does exactly that. With the patience of a loving grandfather, he reaches out his hand, lifts Peter up, and says, "Why did you doubt?" And then he gets into the boat with Peter and the others so that all of them can experience the calm he brings into their midst.

Scripture Reading: Matthew 14:22–33

For Further Reflection
— What are the current storms in your life, and how is Jesus reaching out to you in the midst of them?
— What do you know about Jesus' care for you in the past that would give you encouragement to trust him in the present and the future?

GALLOPING WITH GOD

Our four-year-old granddaughter Maddie gallops when she is happy. This is not a new phenomenon; she's been doing it since she was a toddler. Before she had the verbal skills to tell us when she was happy and when she was sad, we could tell when she was especially happy by her galloping.

Recently, I sat by Maddie through a worship service at our church. I had taken lots of snacks, crayons and paper for coloring, and books to entertain her. But still, at the end of the hour-and-fifteen-minute worship service, Maddie turned to me and said, "That sure was long, Grammy. And it wasn't fun."

I know that church does not always have to be fun. And I know that there are values Maddie is gaining simply by being present in worship—just as I did as a child. She is hearing the stories of faith read from the Scriptures and preached from the pulpit. She is participating in the rituals of baptism and Eucharist that give us identity and shape us as Christians. She is gaining a sense of community and family as she sings hymns and prays prayers in the company of others. But sometimes I wonder: why isn't there more space in worship for children and adults to "gallop with God"?

Surely God would delight in a child galloping up the aisle to receive Communion or skipping around the sanctuary as we sing "Joyful, Joyful, We Adore Thee." Surely God would love it if we adults weren't so uptight in worship and allowed our bodies to show forth our praise as much as we do our lips.

I have certainly worshiped in places where galloping

with God is allowed and even encouraged. Last year, I worshiped in a small, open-air church in rural South Africa, where poor people eke out an existence—most of them working as day laborers for others. Their bodies were constantly in movement. Children stood at the front of the sanctuary, singing, clapping, stomping, and playing rhythm instruments as they led us in song. Adults danced their offerings up to the Communion table, following the children's lead, and even the eldest among them had a sway to their hips and a beat to their steps. When the entire church community gathered afterward for a potluck dinner outside, games of chase surrounded and intersected us. For this faith community, church was not a bit boring. The Sabbath was a day for liberation, joy, and community; a day to be celebrated with movement and song as long as was humanly possible.

Don't get me wrong. I don't want to turn worship into a free for all. I like a good, thoughtful sermon and time out from my hectic week for silent prayer and meditation. But I also long for more space where children and youth and adults can freely gallop with God. Rather than walking back from the Communion table with our eyes cast down, I sometimes feel that we should all be skipping back to our pews—as our organist's daughter regularly does—grateful for the meal we have just shared with one another and the risen Christ. Rather than standing stoically when we sing the hymns, there should be room for rhythm and movement and instrument-playing by the congregation. Rather than somberly engaging in prayer, there should be opportunities—as there are in many Korean American and African American and Pentecostal congregations—for the passionate outpouring of our souls and spirits before God, as we lift our hands toward the heavens and shout out our laments, as well as our thanksgivings, in passionate prayer.

In his letter to the church in Rome, the apostle Paul

says that if people of faith live in the Spirit and the Spirit lives in us, the God "who raised Christ from the dead will give life to your mortal bodies also through his Spirit that dwells in you" (Rom. 8:11b). All I can say is: Bring it on, Spirit! Bring it on.

Scripture Readings: 2 Samuel 6:12–15; Romans 8:11

For Further Reflection
— In 2 Samuel, we read that when King David brought the ark of the covenant into Jerusalem, he "danced before the LORD with all his might." Why do you think many adults today are so reticent to worship God with our whole physical beings?
— Think about the congregations you know that are the most welcoming of children and their fully "embodied" ways of worshiping. What do you learn from them about how we all might worship God more fully with our bodies?

THE CALLING OF A CHILD

When I was a child, the story of the call of Samuel (1 Sam. 3:1–20) was one of my favorite Bible stories. It ranked right up there with the story of Esther (one of the few biblical stories about a strong woman), who risked her life by appearing before the king uninvited and ended up winning freedom for her people, the Jews.

I have always loved that the story of Samuel is about a child who hears God in the night, calling him to be a prophet. This child certainly isn't looking to become a prophet. Indeed, according to the biblical text, he doesn't even "know the LORD" yet (v. 7). So when God calls him in the night by name, he mistakenly thinks that Eli, the old priest he is serving in the temple, is summoning him. It is not until the fourth time the call comes from God, that Samuel, with Eli's instruction, says "Speak, for your servant is listening" (v. 10). And that is when he hears God calling him to tell Eli that the reign of his priesthood is coming to an end because of the blasphemy of his sons. Ouch.

If truth be told, it was not the content of God's call to Samuel that intrigued me as a child. (I'm not even sure I was much aware of it.) It was *that* God called Samuel at all. Here was a kid—sleeping in the temple where the ark of the covenant was housed in the holy of holies and where the "light of the Lord" had not yet gone out—and God actually comes to him in the night and speaks to him by name. "Wow!" I remembering thinking, "If it happened to Samuel, perhaps it can happen to me as well!"

This morning—as I was rereading this beloved old story of Samuel's call again—a new insight dawned on me.

I have long known that God sent the much older, adult Samuel to anoint a new king for Israel after King Saul began displeasing God. But it was not until this morning that I began connecting the dots between Samuel's childhood call to be a prophet and David's childhood call to become a king.

No wonder God sent the prophet Samuel to Bethlehem to anoint David as king over Israel after King Saul began to stray from God's paths (1 Sam. 16:1–13). And no wonder Samuel kept pressing Jesse, who had paraded his seven oldest sons before Samuel first, to bring before him the youngest of the lot, David, who was but a boy tending sheep. Samuel viscerally knew from his experience in the temple that night that God actually calls children to do God's work in the world. And Samuel saw in David, the child whose heart delighted God, the boy who would become the finest king Israel ever had.

I cannot help but wonder how many times children we know and love are called by God, but we have no idea it has happened? How many times do we—unlike Eli in this biblical story—go blithely on our way, not realizing that something momentous has happened between children and God, and then fail to provide them with ears to hear the God who is speaking to them in the night?

I hear a lot of parents talking these days about not wanting to force religion on their children and so not requiring that they attend church or church school. My worry is not what parents are forcing on their children; it's what they are robbing them of by denying them a place in the temple where the holiness of God is experienced, or a seat in church school where they can learn these sacred stories of the faith.

I cannot help but remember the many times in my own childhood when I, sensing the nudge of God, went forward to dedicate my life to Christ at evangelistic revivals (my father was an evangelist at heart, so I often "rode the circuit" with him); or the years when, as a young child, I would sit with my parents at a large church mission conference, listening to the choir singing, "Whom shall I send? And who will go for me?" (based on the story of Isaiah's call in Isa. 6), and with Isaiah I would respond, "Here am I. Please send me!" I am deeply grateful to my parents not only for telling me the story of Samuel but for taking me to places and putting me in situations where I, too, might hear the call of God. They truly believed that God calls children as well as adults, and they helped create opportunities where I, like Samuel of old, might actually hear God calling me in the night—and know that the call was indeed God's.

Samuel's story makes me think about the children I encounter in my life: children I see at church, children of the students I teach, children of friends and family members, my own grandchildren. What a wonder and a gift that God claims young lives as God's very own!

Scripture Reading: 1 Samuel 3:1–20

For Further Reflection
— Did you ever experience the call of God as a child? If so, what form did that call take?
— How did it come to you?
— Who are the children in your life that you might help know the biblical stories of God—including this story about Samuel?

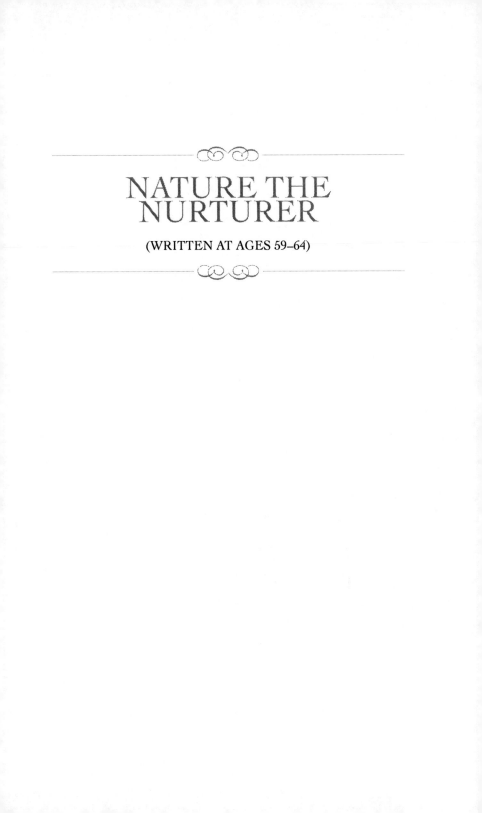

NATURE THE NURTURER

(WRITTEN AT AGES 59–64)

WHY I LOVE MORNING

The poet Mary Oliver, whose work I have long admired, titled one of her books (and poems) *Why I Wake Early*. I knew, the minute I saw the title, that she was a kindred spirit.

This particular morning reminds me of all the reasons I, too, wake early and love mornings. I love the pinks and purples of the sky just before the sun peeks its reddish head over the horizon. I love the stillness of the water and the way in which the geese glide along its surface. I love watching the snowy white egret stand completely still and erect near the edge of the shore, searching patiently for her breakfast. I love watching the swallows fluttering over the marsh, eating bugs as they swoop, their tails shaped like scissors. I love seeing dozens of fishing boats, racing out for their morning's catch. I love hearing the ducks chattering to one another, as they move from cove to cove. And I love feeling the sea breezes caress my cheeks, signaling the promise of a day fresh with possibility.

I also love the solitude of morning, getting up before anyone else in my household and having the world all to myself for a precious hour or two. Having time to commune with God and pour out my thanksgivings and intercessions in my prayer journal. Listening in the stillness to see what promptings of the Spirit will come to me this new day.

My heart in the morning often feels full to overflowing, like the swollen mountain lake I witnessed recently, during a trip to the North Carolina mountains after weeks of rain. Perhaps that is why my favorite hymn since childhood is "Great Is Thy Faithfulness." When my heart is at its fullest and feels as if it must cascade over with wonder and gratitude, it is that hymn that provides my spillway:

Great is thy faithfulness, O God Creator,
There is no shadow of turning with thee,
Thou changest not, thy compassions they fail not,
As thou hast been, thou forever wilt be.

Great is thy faithfulness, great is thy faithfulness,
Morning by morning new mercies I see;
All I have needed, thy hand hath provided,
Great is thy faithfulness, Lord unto me.*

I think many of the psalmists of old must have been morning people, too. When their hearts brimmed full of praise and gratitude, mere prose could not contain it. So they wrote poetry and hymns to pour out their souls in thanksgiving to God:

O LORD, our Sovereign,
    how majestic is your name in all the earth!
                    (Ps. 8:1)

I give you thanks, O LORD, with my whole heart;
    before the gods I sing your praise;
                    (Ps. 138:1)

Bless the LORD, O my soul,
    and all that is within me
    bless [God's] holy name.
                    (Ps. 103:1)

*Thomas Obediah Chisholm, "Great Is Thy Faithfulness," © 1923, Ren. 1951 Hope Publishing Company, Carol Stream, IL 60188. All rights reserved. Used by permission.

One of the psalms, Psalm 148, depicts the whole of creation joining human beings in giving praise to God. Sun and moon, fire and hail, snow and frost, fruit trees and cedars, wild animals and cattle, creeping things and flying birds, even sea monsters! —join in a great thanksgiving chorus. I like to think I hear that chorus as well in the early mornings as the waves gently lap against the shore, the geese stir up the waters with their wings, and the seagulls voice their distinctive cries. Rising sun and parting clouds, rushing minnows and circling ospreys, tall marsh grasses and buzzing bees—let everything that breathes, praise the Lord.

Scripture Reading: Psalm 148

For Further Reflection
— What is the time of day that you love as much as Mary Oliver loves morning?
— When your heart is overflowing with thanksgiving and gratitude, how do you best express it?
— Try writing your own psalm or hymn of praise to thank God for all God has done for you.

A FOG-DRENCHED MORNING

This morning, the world is enshrouded in fog. I cannot see the water that I know is just across the street or any of the boats that are moored there. I can hear the birds, but I can't see them unless they fly right in front of our house. I can hear fishing boats puttering about, and I wonder how they know where they are going.

In the distance, the foghorn sounds. I have grown accustomed to it, and I think of those ancient ships that depended on it to keep them from running up against the rocks. I am told that sailors of old could hear such a horn and know exactly where they were in the water. I find that knowledge only mildly comforting. To be ghosting about in thick fog on a sailing vessel, never completely certain of where the rocks lie, would be frightening.

At the end of 1 Corinthians 13, the apostle Paul likens our knowledge of God in this life to being in thick fog. "For now we see through a glass, darkly; but then face to face: now I know in part; but then shall I know even as also I am known" (1 Cor. 13:12 KJV). The apostle suggests that fog is an ordinary part of life on this earth. It is only when we get to heaven and behold God in all God's glory that we will also attain the sure clarity of spiritual vision that comes with a life lived in complete and harmonious union with our Creator.

I know what the apostle is talking about in terms of this world's realities; and I imagine I am not alone. Have you ever strained hard to see the vocational path ahead of you, only to have it enveloped in pea soup? Have you ever wrestled with a difficult decision you must make without any visible landmarks to guide you? If truth be told, a lot of this life of faith is lived in the mist. We might hear the voice of God in the distance saying, "Do not fear. I am here." But that's about all we have to go on. And so we move forward, hoping and praying we don't run up against the shoals.

I suppose that's what makes faith, faith. We have to move forward with only the voice of God to guide us. We are given no guarantees that we are even headed in the right direction. We seek to discern, as best we can, that one sound that is sure and steady and constant amid all the other sounds clamoring for our attention, and we follow it.

This morning, the sun is beginning to burn off the fog, and shapes that were once invisible are now coming into sight. I suspect that's what heaven will be like. But in the meantime, we strain to hear the voice of God and pray for the courage to follow where it leads us.

Scripture Reading: 1 Corinthians 13:12

For Further Reflection
— What is an area in your life where you feel that you are in the midst of fog and in need of the voice of God to guide you?
— Offer it to God and seek God's guidance for your life.

THE BIRDS

One of the delights of yesterday was being captivated by a bird that I did not remember seeing before. Its colors were extraordinary—a deep purplish-blue cap and back with a Dreamsicle orange breast. I couldn't wait to get home and look it up in my bird book. I knew it must be some exotic species that showed itself only occasionally in the Northeast.

Much to my surprise, I discovered that my exotic bird was actually a barn swallow! Not an extraordinary bird at all, but a common one—a bird I've observed many times near dusk, darting through the sky eating mosquitoes as it goes. However, I'd never seen one up close and standing still before.

Birds have long delighted me. I first started watching them recreationally a number of years ago, when my husband and children gave me a bird feeder for Mother's Day and then put it up where I had a perfect view of it from the sunporch of our New Jersey home. It was there that I first became acquainted with the pointy crest of the gray-tufted titmouse, with the funny way the white-breasted nuthatch hops down trees headfirst, and with the reddish brown coloration of "purple" finches.

When we moved to Connecticut, I was struck by the variety of woodpeckers that inhabited the woods in our area: small downy woodpeckers with black backs, striped wings, and a little red dot on the backs of their heads; "red-bellied" woodpeckers, with their black-and-white-checked backs and flaming red heads. Sometimes, we would see—but more often hear—huge pileated woodpeckers rat-a-tatting like jackhammers as they took large chunks of bark out of dead trees in their quest for food.

Occasionally, a rarer bird would appear at our feeder. I still remember the morning I saw a colorful black and gold Baltimore oriole for the first time; and the day when I rushed to my bird book to identify a feathered species whose beak was shaped a lot like the cardinals I had grown up with in North Carolina but who had a black back, white breast, and red bib around its throat (a rose-breasted grosbeak).

These days it is the sea birds that intrigue me. I love to watch the osprey soaring overhead, with their outstretched crooked wings, looking for fish with which to feed their young. I am intrigued by the migration patterns of the Canadian geese, who nest here every summer, paddling out toward the bay in the evening and back into the marsh eddies in the early morning. The all-black cormorants, like the loons in environs north of here, can stay under water for long periods of time in search of their prey. They remind me of children trying to see how long they can hold their breath when swimming. And then there are the stately white egrets that look as though—with their long arched necks and long thin legs—they should be served their dinner on fine china.

Often when theologians describe God, they use language like "sovereign," "all-powerful," or "omniscient." But nature reminds me that God is also highly *imaginative*. Indeed, at least one theologian (Garrett Green in his book *Imagining God*) has suggested that what it means for us humans to be created in the image of God is that we, too, have the gift of imagination.

I am grateful not only for the fruits of God's imagination that we witness in nature around us but also for those artists through the ages who have tried to capture on canvas or paper or clay or wood something of its beauty through the engagement of their own imaginations. My husband and I once attended a Pennsylvania exhibit of the works of South Carolina artist Grainger McCoy, who has spent his entire adult life carving birds. Almost all of his works depict birds in motion: a hawk preparing to pounce on a snake, a covey of quail arising startled from Low Country grasses, six Carolina parakeets (now extinct) in flight, and, yes, three barn swallows winging their way across the marsh. Each of these birds has been fashioned in meticulous detail by the artist and then set in flight by means of invisible steel and wire. To me there is something wonderfully Godlike not only about nature but also about the people who cherish it and who recreate its glory in their art.

I am grateful that imagination is one of the gifts the Creator of the universe bestowed on us at the beginning of time. And I am grateful for those people who have spent their lives honing that creative gift in order to share it with others.

Scripture Reading: Genesis 1:20–23

For Further Reflection

— How does it change your view of God if you think of God as a highly *imaginative* being? How does it change your view of humanity if you think about God in this way? What gifts of creativity and imagination have you been given, and how do you exercise them?
— What role does nature play in fostering creativity in you?

THE LITTLEST BIRD

This morning, a Sunday, a small sparrow perched outside our dining room window and sang its heart out. I looked at this ordinary, brown bird and marveled that such beautiful, rich melodies could come from this small, unremarkable creature. I was reminded of the song by a Canadian folk group, the Be Good Tanyas, called "The Littlest Birds Sing the Sweetest Songs." This is the second time this summer I have stopped and marveled to see a small bird singing its heart out and filling the world around it with sweet, sweet songs.

I think there's a parable here, though I'm uncertain what it is. Perhaps what this bird is telling us is not to judge by outer appearance but to look and listen to the songs of the heart, as the prophet Samuel did when he tapped David to be king of Israel. I have always loved this biblical story, and the way in which Samuel, with fear and trepidation, goes to Bethlehem, as God instructs him, to anoint a new king for God's people—while Saul is still king. Needless to say, this kind of activity could be viewed as insurrection if tormented King Saul gets wind of it, and Samuel knows that his life is on the line. Nevertheless, he obeys God, travels to the little town of Bethlehem, offers sacrifices there to God, and afterward asks Jesse to bring his sons before him so that he can discern which one God would have as king.

Jesse begins by bringing his oldest son, Eliab, before Samuel, certain that this is the one God would want as a king. But God says to Samuel, "Do not look on his appearance or on the height of his stature, because I have rejected him; *for the LORD does not see as mortals see; they look on the outward appearance, but the LORD looks on the heart"* (1 Sam. 16:7, emphasis added). Jesse then parades six other sons before Samuel, and each time Samuel tells him, "The LORD has not chosen this one." Finally, Samuel says in desperation, "Are all your sons here" (v. 11b)? Jesse replies that the only one remaining is the youngest—a mere kid who is out keeping the sheep. And sure enough, once David is brought before Samuel, God tells Samuel, "Rise and anoint him; for this is the one" (v.12b). So Samuel takes the horn of oil and anoints David in the presence of his older brothers. And we read: "the spirit of the LORD came mightily upon David from that day forward" (v. 13b).

We know that David was not a perfect human being or a perfect king. But it is clear in the testimony of the Scriptures that he was the most beloved king of Israel. He was also a songbird. He loved to play the lyre, which he did in his youth to soothe the spirits of troubled King Saul. He loved to dance, which he did in the streets after his victories in battle. And he must have loved to sing as well, because tradition has attributed the one-hundred-fifty psalms of the Hebrew Scriptures to his pen. He was the littlest and the youngest son, but his songs live on to this day, filling the world with beauty and praise.

Humans look on the outer appearance, but God looks on the heart. How true it is that we humans are inclined to judge by what we see and can easily miss those whose melodies of the heart echo God's own. All too easily we can allow the biggest, the smartest, the most athletic, the richest, the most glamorous to divert our attention away from those who seem insignificant in the eyes of the world but who, in the eyes of God, are the anointed ones.

This day, let us attend to the "least of these," as Jesus constantly did, and listen intently to hear their songs. It may be that they will be the ones who bring us closer to God.

Scripture Reading: 1 Samuel 16:1–13

For Further Reflection
— Think of the unexpected people you know who have
been tapped by God to sing God's own sweet songs and
give thanks for them.

MEETING PETER IN THE BAHAMAS

∞∞

I met the apostle Peter in the Bahamas this past week. He attended a preaching conference for United Methodist pastors I was helping to lead. He traveled from his home on the island of Eleuthera to the capital city of Nassau to be present with fifty other lay leaders and pastors who sacrificially gave up their time and their livelihood for a few days to learn more about preaching. (Only a handful of these pastors are full-time church employees. Most of them work in other vocations while leading churches on the weekends.)

Peter's real name is James. But the more I talked with him and got to know him, the more I knew I was talking with the biblical Peter incarnate.

James is a bone fisherman. That means he goes out each day on his boat and wrestles big, strong bonefish to make a living. He is a rough and unpolished kind of guy—large, dark skinned, with a ready grin. He speaks quickly, and I cannot always decipher all his words. But the essence comes through.

In the workshop he attended with me, he told our group how, before his conversion, he was into a lot of "bad things"—cooking crack cocaine, stealing, participating in gang violence. But then James found Jesus, or I should say, Jesus found James, called him by name, bid him follow, and promised to make him a fisher of people. And now it is the people-fishing, as well as the bone-fishing, that gives joy to this Bahamian.

James' favorite biblical story is the story of the Prodigal Son (Luke 15:11–32). It is clear that he identifies with this renegade child of God, who spent his life in debaucherous living but finally headed home, where he was warmly welcomed and embraced by his loving Father. The embrace of God turned this "Peter's" life around. And he loves to make his witness to any who will listen. In fact, I marveled at how completely unembarrassed this tough guy was in talking about his faith and what it meant to him.

When I asked participants to describe a theological term (such as *sin, grace, holiness*) in language that appeals to one of the senses, "Peter" responded in this manner: "The grace of God is like the sound of gentle waves lapping against the boat when you're out fishing on a sunny day. But God's grace is also with us in the raging storms. Remember where Jesus was in the boat when the storm came up and the other fishermen were afraid? He was sleeping! That's grace, too."

When we were discussing how we might preach forgiveness in a lively and engaging and nonharmful way, James told us his own forgiveness story. He was out in his fishing boat one day, when a pin sheared off of his motor and he was left powerless. When another boat passed by, James and the other fisherman on his boat waved their arms, signaling that they needed help. But the man in the other boat simply looked at them and kept on going. Later that same week, James was out fishing again. On his way back to harbor, he saw a boat that was in trouble and needed a tow. He was headed over to help when one of the other fishermen in his boat said, "Look at who that is! It's the same man who passed us by the other day and refused to help us. I'm not helping tow him!" Whereupon James responded, "Oh, we must help him. That's how we act when we're friends of Jesus. We forgive."

In one of our plenary sessions, a conference leader was asked about how much emotion was appropriate for preachers to display in the pulpit. Specifically, what did she think of people who cry every time they preach?

The leader was addressing that question cautiously and wisely—talking about the need to balance authenticity in our feelings as preachers with an avoidance of emotional manipulation in the pulpit—when "Peter" interrupted her. He stood up in the midst of the group, started talking faster and faster while he was spinning around and around in circles—his arms extended like a helicopter. He told the group (as best I could decipher): "When I tell my story, I cannot contain what Jesus has done for me. I just have to dance and shout and praise my God. God has been so good to me!"

Sometimes when I read the biblical story, I am prone to domesticate it, turning Peter into a well-behaved suburban churchgoer. But James reminded me that God first built the church—and is still building the church today—on the testimony of rough, tough, poorly educated day laborers who have had their lives turned around by an encounter with Jesus. It was to such as Peter that he gave the keys to the church—and is still giving those keys today.

Scripture Reading: Matthew 4:18–22

For Further Reflection
— Reflect on the people Jesus first called to be his disciples. What surprises you about them?
— Where do you see their reality mirrored in current-day disciples of Jesus?

FACING MORTALITY

(WRITTEN AT AGES 61–64)

A TIME TO DIE

When my husband and I were both parish pastors, we used to observe that there were certain seasons of the year when deaths were more likely to occur in our congregations. Late fall was often such a season, as people faced the prospect of hanging on for another long, hard winter. And this month, January, is another. People summon up the will to live through the Christmas holidays and then, having shared time with family and loved ones, are ready to die.

During this past week, I have received word of two family members who have either died or are on the brink of death. I also know of several friends in our congregation and community whose families are keeping vigil, certain that death is imminent.

If there is such a thing, this season of the year seems like a "natural" time to die. The skies are gray, the air (at least in New England) is frigid, and many other living things are either hibernating or buried deep underground, awaiting spring's thaw. 'Tis a season of death, in the literal sense of that term.

Ecclesiastes speaks of "a time to be born, and a time to die" (3:2), and for some—especially for those who have lived long lives and whose bodies are breaking down—winter can be a fitting time to die. It's a time to release their hold on this life and to offer their lives into the hands of a loving, compassionate God.

I don't have a clue what death is actually like (having only heard accounts from those who have had "near-death" experiences). But I think that, at its best, it must be something like falling into a deep sleep. So I applaud the decision of my relatives who decided to opt for surgery for our ninety-one-year-old loved one—despite the considerable risks—rather than allowing him to continue to live in excruciating and unrelenting pain after breaking his hip. If he survives, he will live in less pain. But if he dies, he will die after saying his provisional farewells to those he loves and drifting off into an anesthesia-induced sleep.

And I am relieved that my second relative— who suffered a massive stroke after enjoying a wonderful Christmas visit with her daughter's family—has quickly passed from this world into the next. I find myself hoping that the woman in my congregation, who has been keeping vigil over her lingering spouse for many weeks, will soon know that release as well.

Death is never easy. My niece—who lost her beloved grandfather a year ago—testified to that reality in her Facebook posting yesterday:

> A year ago today I got that phone call, and I can still remember what a punch in the gut it felt like. In the past year I think about my Papa every day, and I have realized that when someone dies they never really leave you. Julia, my daughter, and I say good morning to him every morning by talking to his birdies in his last painting. Circus peanuts in a store always bring a smile to my face; I have had many conversations with him while alone, and I feel his presence every time I walk into his den. I have learned that no matter how long someone is gone . . . you never stop missing them.[*]

Death is never easy. But some deaths are certainly more "timely" than others. In this wintery season of death, I pray that all of those who are enduring death's heartache will also sense the gentle, warm, blanketing love of our God,

[*] Posted by Sarah Tubbs Ramos on Facebook, January 4, 2013.

surrounding them, holding them close, and cradling them as they grieve.

Scripture Reading: Ecclesiastes 3:1–8

For Further Reflection
— Offer prayers to God for all those who are dying, all who are keeping vigil over them, and all who are grieving the anniversaries of deaths in their lives.

DELIVER US FROM CLICHÉS

The author Nora Gallagher has written an article I regularly quote to my introductory preaching classes called "Breaking through the Screen of Cliché." In it she talks about how often the church and its ministers engage in using theological words and phrases in ways that either assume congregants understand their meaning or that are boring and repetitive. Words like *blessing, resurrection, salvation, faith, redemption,* and *forgiveness* are thrown around in trite and facile ways without delving into the depths of their substance and meaning.*

A few days ago, I had lunch with a dear friend who lost her beloved husband less than a year ago. While she readily admits that she is surrounded by a host of loving friends and family who are at her side on this journey through grief, she openly said to me, "I know I am fortunate to have them. But the truth of the matter is, no matter what they do or say, it doesn't take the pain away."

During the course of the conversation, I asked my friend what clichés she had heard since her spouse's death that made her cringe.

"The biggest one," she said, is, "*It must be a part of God's plan*' or '*it must be God's will.*' I don't believe that for a minute. Why would I believe in a God like that?"

She went on to name others:

— "*At least you still have your memories.*' Don't they know

---

*Nora Gallagher, "Breaking through the Screen of Cliché," *Reflections* (Yale Divinity School, 2009), http://reflections.yale.edu/article/how-firm-foundation-churches-face-future/breaking-through-screen-clich, accessed October 11, 2016.

that memories with someone you've loved and lost also hurt?"

— "*'I'm still praying for a miracle'* [spoken just a month before her husband, whose body by that time was eaten up by cancer, died]. What am I supposed to believe? That God goes around saying, 'Yes, I'll answer that prayer and grant a miracle, but no, I'm not going to answer that prayer because it wasn't good enough'?"

— "*'I'm sure it will get better with time.'* That may be true, but it doesn't help me NOW!"

I then asked my friend what had been most helpful to her in her journey through grief, and she cited the presence of a couple of friends who have been willing to go with her to the most painful places and stay there with her, offering encouragement by their silent presence. I was reminded as she spoke of the book of Job, which could probably be subtitled "The Book of Theological Clichés." What Job would have given for a friend who simply sat with him in silence!

I was also reminded of a sermon William Sloane Coffin, then pastor of The Riverside Church in New York City, preached less than two weeks after his beloved twenty-four-year-old son Alexander was killed in a single-car accident. In the sermon, Coffin tells of answering the door at his sister's home soon after Alex's death and being greeted by a woman carrying "about eighteen quiches." As she walked back to the kitchen to deliver her food, she sadly remarked to Coffin, "I just don't understand the will of God."

Coffin reports:

Instantly I was up and in hot pursuit, swarming all over her. "I'll say you don't, lady!" I said. . . . "Do you think it was the will of God that Alex never fixed that lousy windshield wiper of his, that he was probably driving too fast in such a storm, that he probably had had a couple of 'frosties' too many? Do you think it is God's will that there are no streetlights along that stretch of road, and no guard rail separating the road and Boston Harbor?"

For some reason, nothing so infuriates me as the incapacity of seemingly intelligent people to get it through their heads that God doesn't go around this world with his finger on triggers, his fist around knives, his hands on steering wheels. . . . The one thing that should never be said when someone dies is, "It is the will of God." Never do we know enough to say that. My own consolation lies in knowing that it was *not* the will of God that Alex die; that when the waves closed over the sinking car, God's heart was the first of all our hearts to break.*

Toward the end of our lunch together, I asked my friend if she had suffered many such clichés at the hand of her own church. "No," she replied, "my minister and church have been wonderful. What makes church hard is, in many ways, what the church does *right*. My minister came and had Communion with me and my husband three times before he died. You know, when it is just three of you, it is a very intimate thing. So now I can never go to the Communion rail without thinking of those times."

My friend is right. No one can take away the pain of another. But we can stay close to those who are grieving, refusing to fall prey to the temptation of cliché. And by so doing we may become to them Christ incarnate: the Christ who wept with Mary when her brother Lazarus died, the Christ who wept with his family when Alex died, and the Christ who weeps with us still.

*William Sloane Coffin, "Alex's Death," in *The Collected Sermons of William Sloane Coffin: The Riverside Years*, vol. 2 (Louisville: Westminster John Knox Press, 2008), 3–4 (emphasis original).

Scripture Reading: John 11:32–37

For Further Reflection
— What are some theological clichés you have heard that have troubled or offended you?
— Why do you think people of faith sometimes resort to clichés when death occurs?
— As you think about people who have been present for you in helpful ways during times of crisis, what about their presence made it helpful?

EVENSONG

Last evening I went to a choral evensong service that took us to heaven and back. The service had been the dream of a man I know, who is dying of cancer and knows he has only months to live. So he organized it, and he and his pastor planned the service together. He publicized it in the community and invited his family and friends and neighbors to attend.

The service took place in a lovely chapel by the sea where this man has been worshiping since he was a boy. A choir of thirty led us in the sung prayers and responses. We listened to familiar scriptures read, including the traditional funeral text from Revelation 21 about a new heaven and a new earth. We sang (with gusto) evening hymns we rarely have opportunity to sing. And the minister preached a stirring sermon on the Twenty-third Psalm, reminding us that God is not the one who sends evil or suffering or death our way but is the Good Shepherd who walks with us through the valley of the shadow of death and never forsakes us. After his sermon, the choir sang the hauntingly beautiful setting of Psalm 23, composed by John Rutter, who, as we had been reminded in the sermon, knew what it was to lose a beloved child to death.

I have attended many funerals in my life, but rarely have I attended the funeral of someone who is still living. Yet we all knew that is what this was. This was the true funeral—the one this man had planned to minister to his own soul and spirit. And he wanted to attend it himself, experience it himself, and be surrounded by those he knows and loves in the womb of worship before he dies.

There is something profound and powerful about the

church gathering in the very face of imminent death to proclaim our belief in a God of comfort and life. It is as if we are laughing at death, shaking our fists in its face, even as we also acknowledge its devastating reality in our lives and the lives of those we love. And when we are willing to get close to death (a rarity in this death-denying culture) — tiptoeing up to look directly into its abyss—we discover there not emptiness and nothingness but the Good Shepherd, waiting to lead us through the valley of shadows to the green pastures that await us on the other side.

At its very heart, this is what our Christian faith is all about: resurrection, hope, and a God who will never leave us or forsake us in this life or in the life to come. It is the bedrock on which we stand and the belief we boldly proclaim from the rooftops of our hearts.

This year marks the tenth anniversary of a time when I was brought face-to-face with my own mortality during a battle with cancer. I remember being absolutely terrified. I did not want to die any more than my friend wants to die now. But I also remember how the faith of the church upheld and sustained me during those difficult days. I clung, like a drowning woman, to those words of Julian of Norwich, "All shall be well, and all shall be well, and all manner of things shall be well." These days, I am claiming those words on behalf of my friend whose funeral I attended last evening and on behalf of others who are facing life-threatening diseases. The battle is won. The victory is assured. "Where, O death, is your sting?" (1 Cor. 15:55b).

Scripture Readings: Psalm 23; Revelation 21:1–4

For Further Reflection
— What are your fears regarding death—either your own or that of a loved one?

— What assurance do you find in the Scriptures regarding death and God's presence with us during it and after it?
— Where in your life do you need to be reminded of the presence of the Good Shepherd, who will never leave or forsake those who walk through death's deep valleys?

A VIEW OF HEAVEN

⎯⎯⎯⎯⎯⎯ ∽∾ ⎯⎯⎯⎯⎯⎯

This morning, a dear friend of mine, who lost her beloved husband to cancer earlier this month, sent me an email with a one-line question: "What is your vision of heaven?" My friend, a lifelong churchgoer, lives her life on a tightrope between faith and doubt. She would be the first to tell you that faith does not come easily to her. If she's going to teeter one way or the other, it's generally going to be toward doubt. She has no patience with people who don't deal with real day-to-day realities; and she is very aware that a lot of the language the Bible uses to describe heaven—especially in the book of Revelation—is symbolic.

So I knew that what she was asking of me was not that I repeat to her the biblical recounting of a city where streets are paved with gold but that I describe for her the existential reality I envision when I think of heaven. Below is the email I sent her in reply. It is certainly not a definitive view of heaven (people have written tomes on the topic!). But it is my own view. And that was what she was asking me to share with her. Often that is all any person is asking us to share with them—our faith, our beliefs, our hopes. So this is what I wrote to my friend:

It's hard for me to describe my vision of heaven because, if I'm honest, it varies. Probably the constants for me are:

— it's a joyful place (or state of existence) where angels and the heavenly hosts are constantly singing praises to God and to Christ the Lamb;
— it's a place where our loved ones who have died are able to live eternally with God and with all the saints who have gone before them;

— it's a place where, as Revelation tells us, there is no more crying or pain or sadness, and where all that is broken is made whole;
— it's a place where God truly becomes our "all in all" and we know God intimately and completely;
— it's a place where the saints who have gone before us intercede with God on our behalf, and cheer us on as we run the race here below that is set before us (Heb. 11–12), and probably keep on doing good works themselves (We and our children took comfort—when one of their elementary school classmates died some years ago—that their wonderful caregiver when they were little, Sandy Hammond, was there to welcome this child into her loving arms);
— it's a place where we will know and recognize one another and be reunited with our loved ones who have died before us (I truly believe that in the resurrection our personalities live on, so that we will know and be known);
— it's a place where justice and righteousness and equality reign, and the Reign of God is fully realized;
— it's a place where we, too, are transformed and become our best selves (I have told [my husband] Alfred to look for me in the jazz section, because in heaven I'm going to have a voice like Norah Jones and will be singing jazz and blues with great musicians!);
— it's our eternal "home" in the best sense of that term— meaning a place of belonging and peace and safety and infinite love.
— I view heaven overall to be lively and vibrant and beautiful (the promise of the scriptures is that nature, too, will be restored in Christ), and welcoming, and filled with warmth and love. I do not view streets of gold (I think Revelation was using metaphorical language there to speak of its beauty), but I do view that home Christ told us he would prepare for us with "many rooms" and grace sufficient for all.

— If I am honest, I will tell you that there have been times in my past that I have doubted heaven's existence. (Yes, I, too, have my doubts.) I especially remember early in our ministry and about five years into our marriage, when our first pregnancy ended in miscarriage, and I was grieving the loss of that child deeply. But that is where my beloved spouse has been incredibly helpful to me. He not only believes in heaven; he *knows* of its existence in the core of his being, as a priest who has ushered many people into its gates, and as a mystic who sometimes glimpses things I cannot see. I think for him the veil between heaven and earth is incredibly thin. And that has given me great comfort and renewed hope in the promise of heaven.

Scripture Readings: John 14:1–3; Revelation 21:1–7

For Further Reflection
— How would you describe heaven to a friend if asked to do so?
— How does the witness of the Scriptures inform your view?
— What comfort and hope do you find in your heavenly vision?

CPSIA information can be obtained
at www.ICGtesting.com
Printed in the USA
FFOW03n1909081117
43409751-42046FF